7th Grade MATH TEST PREP

Common Core State Standards

teachers' treasures, inc.

Copyright © 2015 Teachers' Treasures Inc.

Printed in the United States of America. All rights reserved. No part of this publication may be reproduced, stored in a retrieval system, or transmitted in any way or by any means (electronic, mechanical, photocopying, recording, or otherwise) without prior written permission from Teachers' Treasures, Inc., with the following exceptions:

Photocopying of student worksheets by a teacher who purchased this publication for his/her own class is permissible, but not for commercial resale. Reproduction of these materials for an entire school, or for a school system, is strictly prohibited. Reproduction of questions or book format by other state or commercial entities is strictly prohibited. Information taken directly from documents published by the Common Core State Standards Initiative is clearly indicated and not copyrighted.

Send all inquiries to:

sales@teacherstreasures.com
http://www.teacherstreasures.com

INTRODUCTION

Our 7th Grade Math Test Prep for Common Core State Standards is an excellent resource to supplement your classroom's curriculum to assess and manage students' understanding of concepts outlined in the Common Core State Standards Initiative. This resource is divided into three sections: Diagnostic, Practice, and Assessment with multiple choice questions in each section. We recommend you use the Diagnostic section as a tool to determine the students' areas that need to be retaught. We also recommend you encourage your students to show their work to determine *how* and *why* the student arrived at an answer. The Practice section should be used to strengthen the students' knowledge by re-testing the standard to ensure comprehension of each standard. To ensure students' apply taught concepts in the classroom, we advise you use the Assessment section as a final test to verify the students' have mastered the standard.

This resource contains over 850 practice problems aligned to the Common Core State Standards. To view the standards, refer to pages *i* through *viii*.

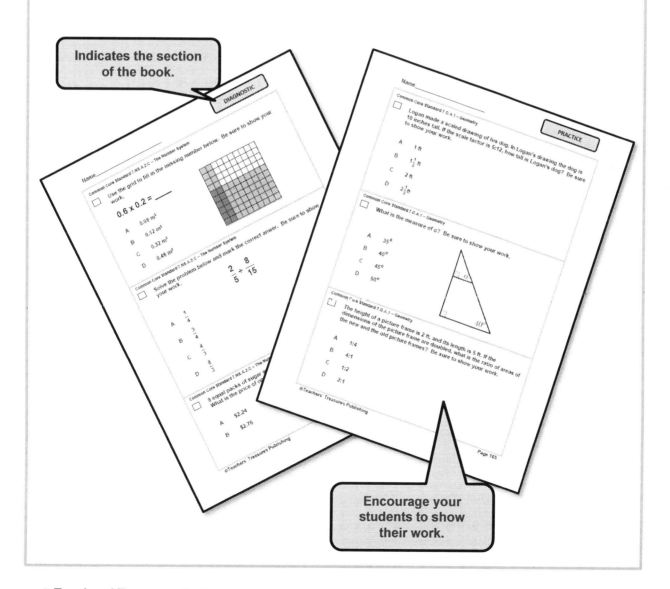

Indicates the section of the book.

Encourage your students to show their work.

© Teachers' Treasures Publishing

TABLE OF CONTENTS

7th Grade Math Test Prep
FOR
Common Core Standards

Grade 7 Mathematics Common Core State Standards .... pages i - viii

Ratios & Proportional Relationships Practice Problems
- 7.RP.A.1............ pages 1 – 8
- 7.RP.A.2.A .... pages 9 – 16
- 7.RP.A.2.B .... pages 17 – 24
- 7.RP.A.2.C .... pages 25 – 32
- 7.RP.A.2.D .... pages 33 – 40
- 7.RP.A.3 .... pages 41 – 48

The Number System Practice Problems
- 7.NS.A.1.A .... pages 49 – 56
- 7.NS.A.1.B .... pages 57 – 64
- 7.NS.A.1.C .... pages 65 – 72
- 7.NS.A.1.D .... pages 73 – 80
- 7.NS.A.2.A .... pages 81 – 88
- 7.NS.A.2.B .... pages 89 – 96
- 7.NS.A.2.C .... pages 97 – 104
- 7.NS.A.2.D .... pages 105 – 112
- 7.NS.A.3 .... pages 113 – 120

Expression & Equations Practice Problems
- 7.EE.A.1 .... pages 121 – 128
- 7.EE.A.2 .... pages 129 – 136
- 7.EE.B.3 .... pages 137 – 144
- 7.EE.B.4.A .... pages 145 – 152
- 7.EE.B.4.B .... pages 153 – 160

Geometry Practice Problems
- 7.G.A.1 .... pages 161 – 168
- 7.G.A.2 .... pages 169 – 176
- 7.G.A.3 .... pages 177 – 184
- 7.G.B.4 .... pages 185 – 192
- 7.G.B.5 .... pages 193 – 200
- 7.G.B.6 .... pages 201 – 208

Statistics & Probability Practice Problems
- 7.SP.A.1 .... pages 209 – 216
- 7.SP.A.2 .... pages 217 – 224
- 7.SP.B.3 .... pages 225 – 232
- 7.SP.B.4 .... pages 233 – 240
- 7.SP.C.5 .... pages 241 – 248
- 7.SP.C.6 .... pages 249 – 256
- 7.SP.C.7.A .... pages 257 – 264
- 7.SP.C.7.B .... pages 265 – 272
- 7.SP.C.8.A .... pages 273 – 280
- 7.SP.C.8.B .... pages 281 – 288
- 7.SP.C.8.C .... pages 289 – 296

Answer Key .... pages 297 – 303

COMMON CORE STATE STANDARDS

Ratios & Proportional Relationships — 7.RP

Analyze proportional relationships and use them to solve real-world and mathematical problems.

CCSS.MATH.CONTENT.7.RP.A.1
Compute unit rates associated with ratios of fractions, including ratios of lengths, areas and other quantities measured in like or different units. *For example, if a person walks 1/2 mile in each 1/4 hour, compute the unit rate as the complex fraction $^{1/2}/_{1/4}$ miles per hour, equivalently 2 miles per hour.*

CCSS.MATH.CONTENT.7.RP.A.2
Recognize and represent proportional relationships between quantities.

> *CCSS.MATH.CONTENT.7.RP.A.2.A*
> Decide whether two quantities are in a proportional relationship, e.g., by testing for equivalent ratios in a table or graphing on a coordinate plane and observing whether the graph is a straight line through the origin.
>
> *CCSS.MATH.CONTENT.7.RP.A.2.B*
> Identify the constant of proportionality (unit rate) in tables, graphs, equations, diagrams, and verbal descriptions of proportional relationships.
>
> *CCSS.MATH.CONTENT.7.RP.A.2.C*
> Represent proportional relationships by equations. *For example, if total cost t is proportional to the number n of items purchased at a constant price p, the relationship between the total cost and the number of items can be expressed as $t = pn$.*
>
> *CCSS.MATH.CONTENT.7.RP.A.2.D*
> Explain what a point (x, y) on the graph of a proportional relationship means in terms of the situation, with special attention to the points $(0, 0)$ and $(1, r)$ where r is the unit rate.

CCSS.MATH.CONTENT.7.RP.A.3
Use proportional relationships to solve multistep ratio and percent problems. Examples: simple interest, tax, markups and markdowns, gratuities and commissions, fees, percent increase and decrease, percent error.

COMMON CORE STATE STANDARDS

The Number System — 7.NS

Apply and extend previous understandings of operations with fractions.

CCSS.MATH.CONTENT.7.NS.A.1
Apply and extend previous understandings of addition and subtraction to add and subtract rational numbers; represent addition and subtraction on a horizontal or vertical number line diagram.

> CCSS.MATH.CONTENT.7.NS.A.1.A
> Describe situations in which opposite quantities combine to make 0. *For example, a hydrogen atom has 0 charge because its two constituents are oppositely charged.*
>
> CCSS.MATH.CONTENT.7.NS.A.1.B
> Understand $p + q$ as the number located a distance $|q|$ from p, in the positive or negative direction depending on whether q is positive or negative. Show that a number and its opposite have a sum of 0 (are additive inverses). Interpret sums of rational numbers by describing real-world contexts.
>
> CCSS.MATH.CONTENT.7.NS.A.1.C
> Understand subtraction of rational numbers as adding the additive inverse, $p - q = p + (-q)$. Show that the distance between two rational numbers on the number line is the absolute value of their difference, and apply this principle in real-world contexts.
>
> CCSS.MATH.CONTENT.7.NS.A.1.D
> Apply properties of operations as strategies to add and subtract rational numbers.

CCSS.MATH.CONTENT.7.NS.A.2
Apply and extend previous understandings of multiplication and division and of fractions to multiply and divide rational numbers.

> CCSS.MATH.CONTENT.7.NS.A.2.A
> Understand that multiplication is extended from fractions to rational numbers by requiring that operations continue to satisfy the properties of operations, particularly the distributive property, leading to products such as $(-1)(-1) = 1$ and

the rules for multiplying signed numbers. Interpret products of rational numbers by describing real-world contexts.

CCSS.MATH.CONTENT.7.NS.A.2.B
Understand that integers can be divided, provided that the divisor is not zero, and every quotient of integers (with non-zero divisor) is a rational number.
If p and q are integers, then $-(p/q) = (-p)/q = p/(-q)$. Interpret quotients of rational numbers by describing real-world contexts.

CCSS.MATH.CONTENT.7.NS.A.2.C
Apply properties of operations as strategies to multiply and divide rational numbers.

CCSS.MATH.CONTENT.7.NS.A.2.D
Convert a rational number to a decimal using long division; know that the decimal form of a rational number terminates in 0s or eventually repeats.

CCSS.MATH.CONTENT.7.NS.A.3
Solve real-world and mathematical problems involving the four operations with rational numbers.

Expressions & Equations   7.EE

Use properties of operations to generate equivalent expressions.

CCSS.MATH.CONTENT.7.EE.A.1
Apply properties of operations as strategies to add, subtract, factor, and expand linear expressions with rational coefficients.

CCSS.MATH.CONTENT.7.EE.A.2
Understand that rewriting an expression in different forms in a problem context can shed light on the problem and how the quantities in it are related. *For example, a + 0.05a = 1.05a means that "increase by 5%" is the same as "multiply by 1.05."*

Solve real-life and mathematical problems using numerical and algebraic expressions and equations.

COMMON CORE STATE STANDARDS

CCSS.MATH.CONTENT.7.EE.B.3
Solve multi-step real-life and mathematical problems posed with positive and negative rational numbers in any form (whole numbers, fractions, and decimals), using tools strategically. Apply properties of operations to calculate with numbers in any form; convert between forms as appropriate; and assess the reasonableness of answers using mental computation and estimation strategies. *For example: If a woman making $25 an hour gets a 10% raise, she will make an additional 1/10 of her salary an hour, or $2.50, for a new salary of $27.50. If you want to place a towel bar 9 3/4 inches long in the center of a door that is 27 1/2 inches wide, you will need to place the bar about 9 inches from each edge; this estimate can be used as a check on the exact computation.*

CCSS.MATH.CONTENT.7.EE.B.4
Use variables to represent quantities in a real-world or mathematical problem, and construct simple equations and inequalities to solve problems by reasoning about the quantities.

CCSS.MATH.CONTENT.7.EE.B.4.A
Solve word problems leading to equations of the form $px + q = r$ and $p(x + q) = r$, where p, q, and r are specific rational numbers. Solve equations of these forms fluently. Compare an algebraic solution to an arithmetic solution, identifying the sequence of the operations used in each approach. *For example, the perimeter of a rectangle is 54 cm. Its length is 6 cm. What is its width?*

CCSS.MATH.CONTENT.7.EE.B.4.B
Solve word problems leading to inequalities of the form $px + q > r$ or $px + q < r$, where p, q, and r are specific rational numbers. Graph the solution set of the inequality and interpret it in the context of the problem. *For example: As a salesperson, you are paid $50 per week plus $3 per sale. This week you want your pay to be at least $100. Write an inequality for the number of sales you need to make, and describe the solutions.*

Geometry 7.G

Draw construct, and describe geometrical figures and describe the relationships between them.

CCSS.MATH.CONTENT.7.G.A.1
Solve problems involving scale drawings of geometric figures, including computing

COMMON CORE STATE STANDARDS

actual lengths and areas from a scale drawing and reproducing a scale drawing at a different scale.

CCSS.MATH.CONTENT.7.G.A.2
Draw (freehand, with ruler and protractor, and with technology) geometric shapes with given conditions. Focus on constructing triangles from three measures of angles or sides, noticing when the conditions determine a unique triangle, more than one triangle, or no triangle.

Solve real-life and mathematical problems involving angle measure, area, surface area, and volume.

CCSS.MATH.CONTENT.7.G.B.4
Know the formulas for the area and circumference of a circle and use them to solve problems; give an informal derivation of the relationship between the circumference and area of a circle.

CCSS.MATH.CONTENT.7.G.B.5
Use facts about supplementary, complementary, vertical, and adjacent angles in a multi-step problem to write and solve simple equations for an unknown angle in a figure.

CCSS.MATH.CONTENT.7.G.B.6
Solve real-world and mathematical problems involving area, volume and surface area of two- and three-dimensional objects composed of triangles, quadrilaterals, polygons, cubes, and right prisms.

Statistics & Probability   7.SP

Use random sampling to draw inferences about a population.

CCSS.MATH.CONTENT.7.SP.A.1
Understand that statistics can be used to gain information about a population by examining a sample of the population; generalizations about a population from a sample are valid only if the sample is representative of that population. Understand that random sampling tends to produce representative samples and support valid inferences.

COMMON CORE STATE STANDARDS

<u>CCSS.MATH.CONTENT.7.SP.A.2</u>
Use data from a random sample to draw inferences about a population with an unknown characteristic of interest. Generate multiple samples (or simulated samples) of the same size to gauge the variation in estimates or predictions. *For example, estimate the mean word length in a book by randomly sampling words from the book; predict the winner of a school election based on randomly sampled survey data. Gauge how far off the estimate or prediction might be.*

Draw informal comparative inferences about two populations.

<u>CCSS.MATH.CONTENT.7.SP.B.3</u>
Informally assess the degree of visual overlap of two numerical data distributions with similar variabilities, measuring the difference between the centers by expressing it as a multiple of a measure of variability. *For example, the mean height of players on the basketball team is 10 cm greater than the mean height of players on the soccer team, about twice the variability (mean absolute deviation) on either team; on a dot plot, the separation between the two distributions of heights is noticeable.*

<u>CCSS.MATH.CONTENT.7.SP.B.4</u>
Use measures of center and measures of variability for numerical data from random samples to draw informal comparative inferences about two populations. *For example, decide whether the words in a chapter of a seventh-grade science book are generally longer than the words in a chapter of a fourth-grade science book.*

Investigate chance processes and develop, use, and evaluate probability models.

<u>CCSS.MATH.CONTENT.7.SP.C.5</u>
Understand that the probability of a chance event is a number between 0 and 1 that expresses the likelihood of the event occurring. Larger numbers indicate greater likelihood. A probability near 0 indicates an unlikely event, a probability around 1/2 indicates an event that is neither unlikely nor likely, and a probability near 1 indicates a likely event.

<u>CCSS.MATH.CONTENT.7.SP.C.6</u>
Approximate the probability of a chance event by collecting data on the chance process that produces it and observing its long-run relative frequency, and predict the approximate relative frequency given the probability. *For example, when rolling a*

number cube 600 times, predict that a 3 or 6 would be rolled roughly 200 times, but probably not exactly 200 times.

CCSS.MATH.CONTENT.7.SP.C.7
Develop a probability model and use it to find probabilities of events. Compare probabilities from a model to observed frequencies; if the agreement is not good, explain possible sources of the discrepancy.

> CCSS.MATH.CONTENT.7.SP.C.7.A
> Develop a uniform probability model by assigning equal probability to all outcomes, and use the model to determine probabilities of events. *For example, if a student is selected at random from a class, find the probability that Jane will be selected and the probability that a girl will be selected.*

> CCSS.MATH.CONTENT.7.SP.C.7.B
> Develop a probability model (which may not be uniform) by observing frequencies in data generated from a chance process. *For example, find the approximate probability that a spinning penny will land heads up or that a tossed paper cup will land open-end down. Do the outcomes for the spinning penny appear to be equally likely based on the observed frequencies?*

CCSS.MATH.CONTENT.7.SP.C.8
Find probabilities of compound events using organized lists, tables, tree diagrams, and simulation.

> CCSS.MATH.CONTENT.7.SP.C.8.A
> Understand that, just as with simple events, the probability of a compound event is the fraction of outcomes in the sample space for which the compound event occurs.

> CCSS.MATH.CONTENT.7.SP.C.8.B
> Represent sample spaces for compound events using methods such as organized lists, tables and tree diagrams. For an event described in everyday language (e.g., "rolling double sixes"), identify the outcomes in the sample space which compose the event.

COMMON CORE STATE STANDARDS

CCSS.MATH.CONTENT.7.SP.C.8.C

Design and use a simulation to generate frequencies for compound events. *For example, use random digits as a simulation tool to approximate the answer to the question: If 40% of donors have type A blood, what is the probability that it will take at least 4 donors to find one with type A blood?*

MATHEMATICS CHART

LENGTH

Metric

1 kilometer = 1000 meters
1 meter = 100 centimeters
1 centimeter = 10 millimeters

Customary

1 yard = 3 feet
1 foot = 12 inches

CAPACITY & VOLUME

Metric

1 liter = 1000 milliliters

Customary

1 gallon = 4 quarts
1 gallon = 128 ounces
1 quart = 2 pints
1 pint = 2 cups
1 cup = 8 ounces

MASS & WEIGHT

Metric

1 kilogram = 1000 grams
1 gram = 1000 milligrams

Customary

1 ton = 2000 pounds
1 pound = 16 ounces

TIME

1 year = 365 days

1 year = 12 months

1 year = 52 weeks

1 week = 7 days

1 day = 24 hours

1 hour = 60 minutes

1 minute = 60 seconds

MATHEMATICS CHART

Perimeter	square	$P = 4s$
	rectangle	$P = 2l + 2w$ or $P = 2(l + w)$
Circumference	circle	$C = 2\pi r$ or $C = \pi d$
Area	square	$A = s^2$
	rectangle	$A = lw$ or $A = bh$
	triangle	$A = \frac{1}{2}bh$ or $A = \frac{bh}{2}$
	trapezoid	$A = \frac{1}{2}(b_1 + b_2)h$ or $A = \frac{(b_1 + b_2)h}{2}$
	circle	$A = \pi r^2$
Volume	cube	$V = s^3$
	rectangular prism	$V = lwh$
Pi	π	$\pi \approx 3.14$ or $\pi \approx \frac{22}{7}$

Name_____

DIAGNOSTIC

Common Core Standard 7.RP.A.1 – Ratios & Proportional Relationships

☐ How many 1/8 l glasses of juice can you pour from a 1/2 l bottle of juice? Be sure to show your work.

- A   2
- B   4
- C   6
- D   8

Common Core Standard 7.RP.A.1 – Ratios & Proportional Relationships

☐ The area of the rectangular piece of carpet is 3/4 m^2. How many pieces of carpet are needed to cover the floor with the area of 3/2 m^2? Be sure to show your work.

- A   2
- B   3
- C   4
- D   6

Common Core Standard 7.RP.A.1 – Ratios & Proportional Relationships

☐ Rufus the Dog runs 1/2 mile in a minute. What is the average speed of the dog per hour? Be sure to show your work.

- A   2 mi/h
- B   30 mi/h
- C   60 mi/h
- D   120 mi/h

©Teachers' Treasures Publishing

Name_____

DIAGNOSTIC

Common Core Standard 7.RP.A.1 – Ratios & Proportional Relationships

☐ **How many 1/10 kg cones of ice cream can you make from a 1/2 kg pack of ice cream? Be sure to show your work.**

    A   20

    B   10

    C   5

    D   2

Common Core Standard 7.RP.A.1 – Ratios & Proportional Relationships

☐ **The area of a tile is 1/9 yd^2. How many tiles are needed to cover the walkway with the area of 2/3 yd^2? Be sure to show your work.**

    A   2

    B   3

    C   6

    D   9

Common Core Standard 7.RP.A.1 – Ratios & Proportional Relationships

☐ **A clown fish swims 1/3 mile in 5 minutes. What is the average speed of a clown fish per hour? Be sure to show your work.**

    A   3 mi/h

    B   4 mi/h

    C   12 mi/h

    D   15 mi/h

©Teachers' Treasures Publishing

Name_____

PRACTICE

Common Core Standard 7.RP.A.1 – Ratios & Proportional Relationships

☐ How many 1/20 m pieces of wood can you cut from a 1/4 m wood stick? Be sure to show your work.

- A   5
- B   10
- C   20
- D   80

Common Core Standard 7.RP.A.1 – Ratios & Proportional Relationships

☐ The area of the rectangular piece of fleece is 1/6 ft^2. How many pieces of fleece are needed to cover a sitting area of 1/2 ft^2? Be sure to show your work.

- A   2
- B   3
- C   4
- D   12

Common Core Standard 7.RP.A.1 – Ratios & Proportional Relationships

☐ A bee flies 1/4 mile per minute. What is the average speed of a bee per hour? Be sure to show your work.

- A   4 mi/h
- B   9 mi/h
- C   12 mi/h
- D   15 mi/h

©Teachers' Treasures Publishing

Name_____

PRACTICE

Common Core Standard 7.RP.A.1 – Ratios & Proportional Relationships

☐ **John and Greg built a tower of cards the height of which is 2/5 m. Each level of the tower is 1/10 m high. How many levels does the tower have? Be sure to show your work.**

A   4

B   5

C   10

D   20

Common Core Standard 7.RP.A.1 – Ratios & Proportional Relationships

☐ **Anne and Lisa are making a sign with an area of 1/2 ft^2. Using self-adhesive pads with an area of 1/8 ft^2 each, how many pads will Anne and Lisa need to cover the sign? Be sure to show your work.**

A   2

B   4

C   8

D   16

Common Core Standard 7.RP.A.1 – Ratios & Proportional Relationships

☐ **Kyle walks 1/2 km in 10 minutes. What is Kyle's average speed per hour? Be sure to show your work.**

A   3 km/h

B   5 km/h

C   10 km/h

D   20 km/h

Name_____

PRACTICE

Common Core Standard 7.RP.A.1 – Ratios & Proportional Relationships

☐ Joshua paid 1/2 a dollar for a pint of mineral water. How much would he pay for a gallon? (1 pint = 1/8 gallon) Be sure to show your work.

A $2

B $4

C $8

D $16

Common Core Standard 7.RP.A.1 – Ratios & Proportional Relationships

☐ The area of a piece of parquet is 1/18 ft². How many pieces of parquet are needed to cover the floor with an area of 1/3 ft²? Be sure to show your work.

A   6

B   15

C   21

D   54

Common Core Standard 7.RP.A.1 – Ratios & Proportional Relationships

☐ A snail crawls 1/3 yd in 1/6 hour. What is the average speed of a snail per hour? Be sure to show your work.

A   2 yd/h

B   3 yd/h

C   9 yd/h

D   18 yd/h

©Teachers' Treasures Publishing

Name_____

PRACTICE

Common Core Standard 7.RP.A.1 – Ratios & Proportional Relationships

☐ **An inch of the lace ribbon costs 3/4 of a dollar. How much would you pay for 1 yard of the lace ribbon? (1 inch = 1/12 yard)   Be sure to show your work.**

- A $3
- B $4
- C $9
- D $12

Common Core Standard 7.RP.A.1 – Ratios & Proportional Relationships

☐ **The area of the bottom side of matchbox is 1/24 ft^2. How many matchboxes are needed to cover the area of 1/2 ft^2? Be sure to show your work.**

- A   12
- B   22
- C   26
- D   48

Common Core Standard 7.RP.A.1 – Ratios & Proportional Relationships

☐ **Kiera rides 1/2 mile in 1/12 hour on her bike. What is the average speed Kiera rides her bike per hour? Be sure to show your work.**

- A   3 mi/h
- B   6 mi/h
- C   7 mi/h
- D   10 mi/h

©Teachers' Treasures Publishing

Name _____

ASSESSMENT

Common Core Standard 7.RP.A.1 – Ratios & Proportional Relationships

☐ How many 1/4 kg serving plates are needed to serve 4 1/2 kg of cake? Be sure to show your work.

  A 4

  B 8

  C 9

  D 18

Common Core Standard 7.RP.A.1 – Ratios & Proportional Relationships

☐ The area of a piece of scrap paper is 1/15 yd². How many pieces of scrap paper are needed to cover an area of 1/3 yd² in a scrap book? Be sure to show your work.

  A 5

  B 12

  C 18

  D 45

Common Core Standard 7.RP.A.1 – Ratios & Proportional Relationships

☐ Marnie drives 1/2 a mile in 1/2 a minute in her car. What is Marnie's average speed per hour? Be sure to show your work.

  A 20 mi/h

  B 40 mi/h

  C 60 mi/h

  D 80 mi/h

©Teachers' Treasures Publishing

Name_____

ASSESSMENT

Common Core Standard 7.RP.A.1 – Ratios & Proportional Relationships

☐ **The city bus route is 5 1/2 miles long. The bus stops are at every 1/4 mile. How many bus stops are there en route? Be sure to show your work.**

    A   4

    B   5

    C   11

    D   22

Common Core Standard 7.RP.A.1 – Ratios & Proportional Relationships

☐ **The area of one tile is 1/72 yd^2. How many tiles are needed to cover the bathroom floor with an area of 10 1/2 yd^2? Be sure to show your work.**

    A   198

    B   378

    C   396

    D   756

Common Core Standard 7.RP.A.1 – Ratios & Proportional Relationships

☐ **A snake passes 1/6 m in 1/2 a minute. What is the average speed of the snake per hour? Be sure to show your work.**

    A   3 m/h

    B   6 m/h

    C   12 m/h

    D   20 m/h

©Teachers' Treasures Publishing

Name_____

DIAGNOSTIC

Common Core Standard 7.RP.A.2.A – Ratios & Proportional Relationships

☐ Which of the answers is equivalent to the ratio below? Be sure to show your work.

6 boys for every 4 girls

A   8 boys for every 6 girls

B   12 boys for every 8 girls

C   4 boys for every 6 girls

D   3 boys for every 8 girls

Common Core Standard 7.RP.A.2.A – Ratios & Proportional Relationships

☐ Which ratio forms a proportion with 10/12? Be sure to show your work.

A   5/6

B   6/5

C   12/10

D   12/14

Common Core Standard 7.RP.A.2.A – Ratios & Proportional Relationships

☐ Fill in the missing number so that the quantities in the table below are in a proportional relationship. Be sure to show your work.

Dogs	1	2	3	4
Legs	4	8		16

A   10

B   12

C   14

D   15

Name_____

DIAGNOSTIC

Common Core Standard 7.RP.A.2.A – Ratios & Proportional Relationships

☐ **Look at the graph below. Which line represents directly proportional relationship? Be sure to show your work.**

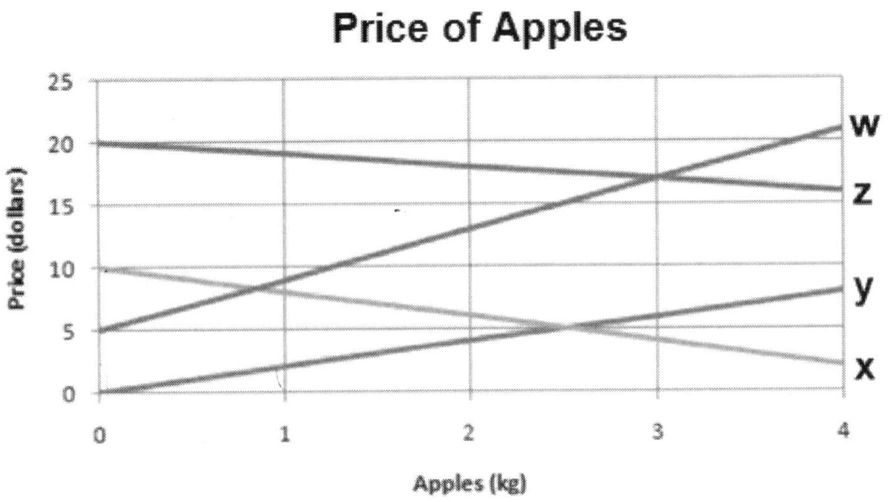

Price of Apples

A	x	C	z
B	y	D	w

Common Core Standard 7.RP.A.2.A – Ratios & Proportional Relationships

☐ **Which ratio is equivalent to 2:6? Be sure to show your work.**

A	6:2	C	1:3
B	3:1	D	1:5

Common Core Standard 7.RP.A.2.A – Ratios & Proportional Relationships

☐ **Look at the table below. Are the quantities in a proportional relationship? Be sure to show your work.**

Wheels	6	8	10	12
Bikes	3	4	5	6

A	yes	C	partially yes
B	no	D	mostly no

©Teachers' Treasures Publishing

Name_____

PRACTICE

Common Core Standard 7.RP.A.2.A – Ratios & Proportional Relationships

☐ Which of the following answers is equivalent to the ratio below? Be sure to show your work.

3 spoons of sugar for every 5 cups of coffee

A   2 spoons of sugar for every 4 cups of coffee

B   4 spoons of sugar for every 6 cup of coffee

C   6 spoons of sugar for every 10 cups of coffee

D   10 spoons of sugar for every 16 cups of coffee

Common Core Standard 7.RP.A.2.A – Ratios & Proportional Relationships

☐ Which ratio forms a proportion with 12/8? Be sure to show your work.

A   3/2

B   10/6

C   14/10

D   8/12

Common Core Standard 7.RP.A.2.A – Ratios & Proportional Relationships

☐ Fill in the missing number so that the quantities in the table below are in a proportional relationship. Be sure to show your work.

Bottle	2		6	8
Liters	3	6	9	12

A   3

B   4

C   5

D   6

©Teachers' Treasures Publishing

Name_____

PRACTICE

Common Core Standard 7.RP.A.2.A – Ratios & Proportional Relationships

☐ **Look at the graph below. Are the quantities in a proportional relationship? Be sure to show your work.**

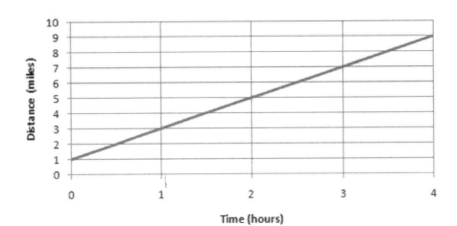

A   yes   C   partially yes

B   no   D   mostly no

Common Core Standard 7.RP.A.2.A – Ratios & Proportional Relationships

☐ **Which ratio is equivalent to 6:3? Be sure to show your work.**

A   1:2   C   2:1

B   1:3   D   3:1

Common Core Standard 7.RP.A.2.A – Ratios & Proportional Relationships

☐ **Look at the table below. Are the quantities in a proportional relationship? Be sure to show your work.**

Cages	1	2	3	4
Parrots	3	5	7	9

A   yes   C   partially no

B   mostly yes   D   no

Name_____

PRACTICE

Common Core Standard 7.RP.A.2.A – Ratios & Proportional Relationships

☐ Which of the following ratios is equivalent to the ratio below? Be sure to show your work.

4 dogs for every 16 bones

A   8 dogs for every 20 bones

B   2 dogs for every 14 bones

C   8 dogs for every 12 bones

D   2 dogs for every 8 bones

Common Core Standard 7.RP.A.2.A – Ratios & Proportional Relationships

☐ Which ratio forms a proportion with 3/5? Be sure to show your work.

A   4/6

B   5/7

C   6/10

D   7/12

Common Core Standard 7.RP.A.2.A – Ratios & Proportional Relationships

☐ Fill in the missing number so that the quantities in the table below are in a proportional relationship. Be sure to show your work.

Petals	4	8	12	
Flowers	1	2	3	4

A   14

B   16

C   18

D   20

©Teachers' Treasures Publishing

Name_____

PRACTICE

Common Core Standard 7.RP.A.2.A – Ratios & Proportional Relationships

☐ **Look at the graph below. Which line represents directly proportional relationship? Be sure to show your work.**

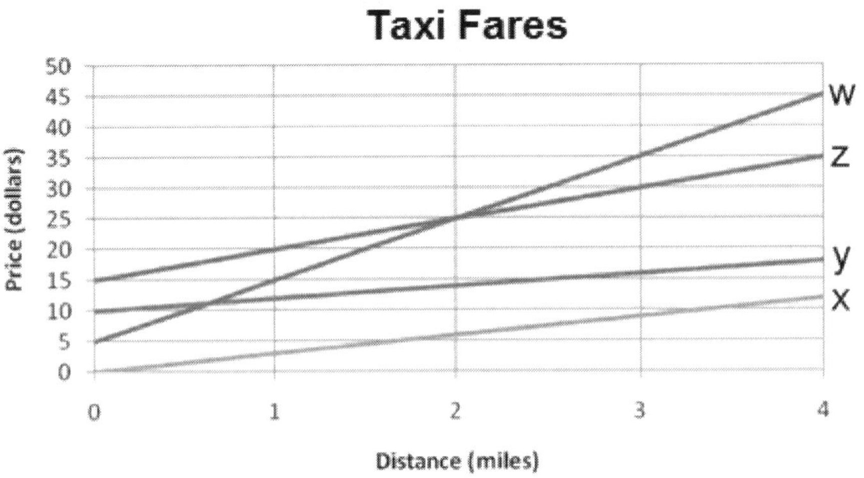

Taxi Fares

A	x	C	z
B	y	D	w

Common Core Standard 7.RP.A.2.A – Ratios & Proportional Relationships

☐ **Which ratio is equivalent to 4:10? Be sure to show your work.**

A	2:8	C	2:5
B	10:4	D	1:5

Common Core Standard 7.RP.A.2.A – Ratios & Proportional Relationships

☐ **Look at the table below. Are the quantities in a proportional relationship? Be sure to show your work.**

Yards	3	6	12	15
Feet	1	2	4	5

A	mostly yes	C	partially no
B	no	D	yes

©Teachers' Treasures Publishing

Name_____

ASSESSMENT

Common Core Standard 7.RP.A.2.A – Ratios & Proportional Relationships

☐ Which of the following ratios is equivalent to the ratio below? Be sure to show your work.

10 pets for every 6 owners

A   8 pets for every 4 owners

B   6 pets for every 2 owners

C   5 pets for every 3 owners

D   6 pets for every 10 owners

Common Core Standard 7.RP.A.2.A – Ratios & Proportional Relationships

☐ Which ratio forms a proportion with 20/15? Be sure to show your work.

A   25/20

B   4/3

C   5/4

D   15/20

Common Core Standard 7.RP.A.2.A – Ratios & Proportional Relationships

☐ Fill in the missing number so that the quantities in the table below are in a proportional relationship. Be sure to show your work.

Seats	5	25	35	40
Cars		5	7	8

A   1

B   2

C   3

D   4

©Teachers' Treasures Publishing

Name_____

ASSESSMENT

Common Core Standard 7.RP.A.2.A – Ratios & Proportional Relationships

☐   **Look at the graph below. Are the quantities in a proportional relationship? Be sure to show your work.**

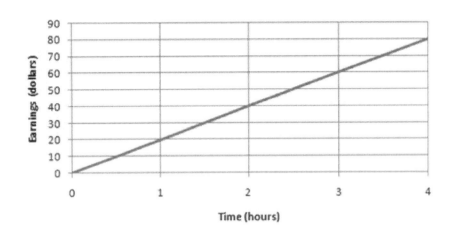

A   yes

B   mostly no

C   partially yes

D   no

Common Core Standard 7.RP.A.2.A – Ratios & Proportional Relationships

☐   **Which ratio is equivalent to 16:12? Be sure to show your work.**

A   12:16

B   4:3

C   10:4

D   3:4

Common Core Standard 7.RP.A.2.A – Ratios & Proportional Relationships

☐   **Look at the table below. Are the quantities in a proportional relationship? Be sure to show your work.**

Pigs	2	4	5	7
Height (lbs)	80	120	200	280

A   yes

B   mostly yes

C   partially no

D   no

©Teachers' Treasures Publishing

Name_____

DIAGNOSTIC

Common Core Standard 7.RP.A.2.B – Ratios & Proportional Relationships

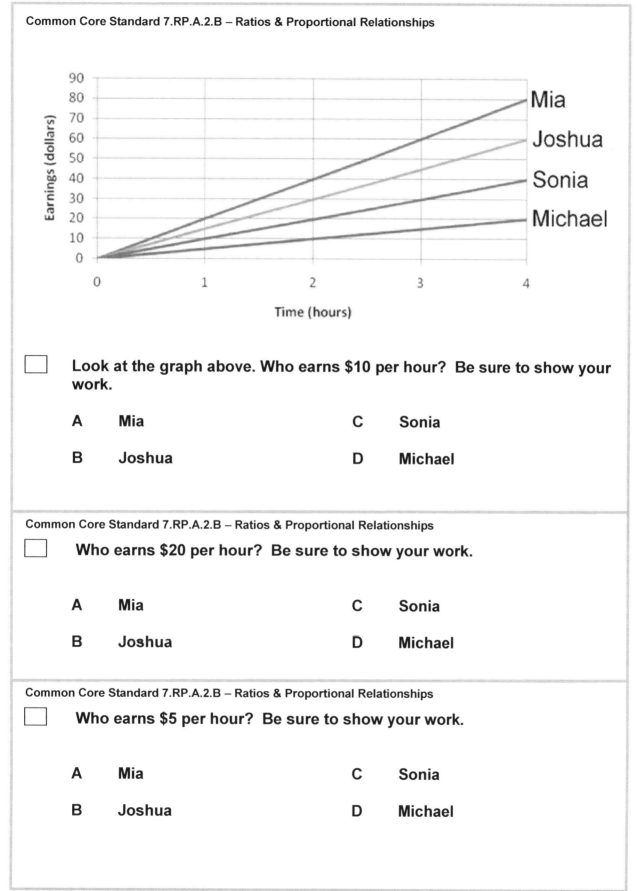

☐ Look at the graph above. Who earns $10 per hour? Be sure to show your work.

A   Mia
B   Joshua
C   Sonia
D   Michael

Common Core Standard 7.RP.A.2.B – Ratios & Proportional Relationships

☐ Who earns $20 per hour? Be sure to show your work.

A   Mia
B   Joshua
C   Sonia
D   Michael

Common Core Standard 7.RP.A.2.B – Ratios & Proportional Relationships

☐ Who earns $5 per hour? Be sure to show your work.

A   Mia
B   Joshua
C   Sonia
D   Michael

Name_____

DIAGNOSTIC

Common Core Standard 7.RP.A.2.B – Ratios & Proportional Relationships

Spiders	3	5		10
Legs	24		48	80

☐ The quantities in the table above are in a proportional relationship. How many legs does a spider have? Be sure to show your work.

A   2

B   4

C   6

D   8

Common Core Standard 7.RP.A.2.B – Ratios & Proportional Relationships

☐ Using the same table, fill in the missing value in the first row.

A   6

B   7

C   8

D   9

Common Core Standard 7.RP.A.2.B – Ratios & Proportional Relationships

☐ Fill in the missing value in the second row.

A   30

B   35

C   40

D   45

©Teachers' Treasures Publishing

Name_____

PRACTICE

Common Core Standard 7.RP.A.2.B – Ratios & Proportional Relationships

☐ The bus passed 120 miles in 2 hours and 180 miles in 3 hours. What is the average speed of the bus? Be sure to show your work.

- A 50 mi/h
- B 55 mi/h
- C 60 mi/h
- D 65 mi/h

Common Core Standard 7.RP.A.2.B – Ratios & Proportional Relationships

☐ 4 packs of soda contain 24 bottles, and 6 packs of soda contain 36 bottles. How many bottles are there in a pack? Be sure to show your work.

- A 4
- B 6
- C 10
- D 12

Common Core Standard 7.RP.A.2.B – Ratios & Proportional Relationships

☐ 6 yards are equal to 18 feet, and 8 yards are equal to 24 feet. How many feet are there in a yard? Be sure to show your work.

- A 3
- B 4
- C 5
- D 6

©Teachers' Treasures Publishing

Name_____

PRACTICE

Common Core Standard 7.RP.A.2.B – Ratios & Proportional Relationships

☐ **The equation $p = 7t$ represents the number of players p, reflected by the number of football teams t. How many players are there in a football team? Be sure to show your work.**

    A   5

    B   7

    C   11

    D   14

Common Core Standard 7.RP.A.2.B – Ratios & Proportional Relationships

☐ **The equation $w = 4c$ represents the number of wheels w, reflected by the number of cars c. How many wheels does a car have? Be sure to show your work.**

    A   2

    B   3

    C   4

    D   6

Common Core Standard 7.RP.A.2.B – Ratios & Proportional Relationships

☐ **The equation $w = 3r$ represents the number of windows w, reflected by the number of rooms r. How many windows does a room have?**

    A   3

    B   4

    C   5

    D   6

©Teachers' Treasures Publishing

Common Core Standard 7.RP.A.2.B – Ratios & Proportional Relationships

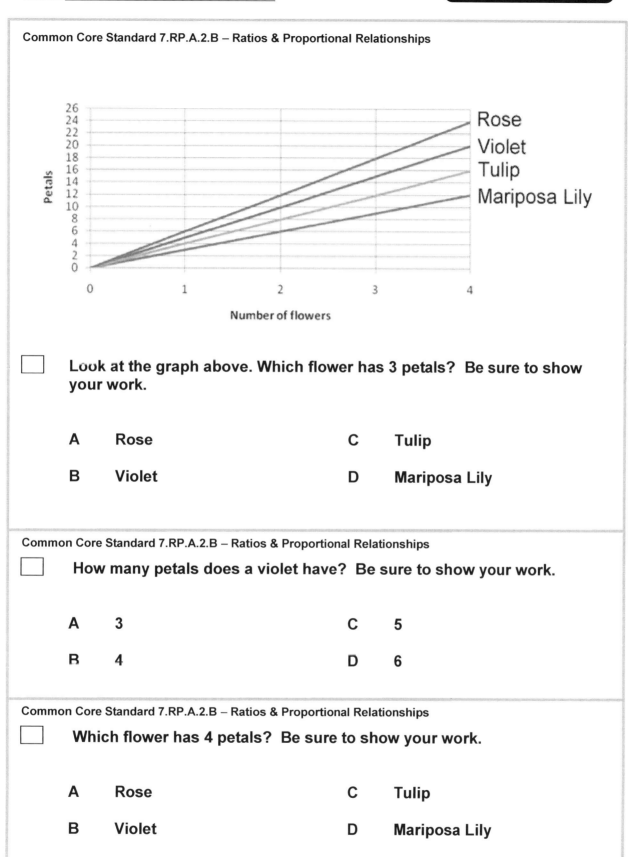

☐ Look at the graph above. Which flower has 3 petals? Be sure to show your work.

A   Rose C   Tulip

B   Violet D   Mariposa Lily

Common Core Standard 7.RP.A.2.B – Ratios & Proportional Relationships

☐ How many petals does a violet have? Be sure to show your work.

A   3 C   5

B   4 D   6

Common Core Standard 7.RP.A.2.B – Ratios & Proportional Relationships

☐ Which flower has 4 petals? Be sure to show your work.

A   Rose C   Tulip

B   Violet D   Mariposa Lily

Name_____

PRACTICE

Common Core Standard 7.RP.A.2.B – Ratios & Proportional Relationships

Bear paws		8	15	20
Claws	15	40		100

☐ **The quantities in the table above are in a proportional relationship. How many claws does a bear paw have? Be sure to show your work.**

    A   3

    B   4

    C   5

    D   6

Common Core Standard 7.RP.A.2.B – Ratios & Proportional Relationships

☐ **Referring to the same table, fill in the missing value in the first row.**

    A   2

    B   3

    C   4

    D   5

Common Core Standard 7.RP.A.2.B – Ratios & Proportional Relationships

☐ **Fill in the missing value in the second row.**

    A   60

    B   65

    C   70

    D   75

Name_____

ASSESSMENT

Common Core Standard 7.RP.A.2.B – Ratios & Proportional Relationships

☐   **Sarah walks 8 miles in 4 hours and 12 miles in 6 hours. What is her average speed? Be sure to show your work.**

    A   2 mi/h

    B   4 mi/h

    C   6 mi/h

    D   8 mi/h

Common Core Standard 7.RP.A.2.B – Ratios & Proportional Relationships

☐   **5 flies have 20 wings, and 7 flies have 28 wings. How many wings does a fly have?   Be sure to show your work.**

    A   2

    B   4

    C   6

    D   8

Common Core Standard 7.RP.A.2.B – Ratios & Proportional Relationships

☐   **3 clovers have 9 petals, and 5 clovers have 15 petals. How many petals does a clover have? Be sure to show your work.**

    A   3

    B   4

    C   5

    D   6

Name_____

ASSESSMENT

Common Core Standard 7.RP.A.2.B – Ratios & Proportional Relationships

☐ The equation $w = 4r$ represents the number of walls, reflected by the number of rooms r. How many walls does a room have? Be sure to show your work.

    A   2

    B   3

    C   4

    D   5

Common Core Standard 7.RP.A.2.B – Ratios & Proportional Relationships

☐ The equation $w = 4b$ represents the weight w, reflected by the number of bags b. How much does a bag weigh? Be sure to show your work.

    A   2 lb

    B   3 lb

    C   4 lb

    D   6 lb

Common Core Standard 7.RP.A.2.B – Ratios & Proportional Relationships

☐ The equation $s = 6p$ represents the number of sides s, reflected by the number of polygons p. Which polygon is represented by the equation? Be sure to show your work.

    A   Square

    B   Pentagon

    C   Hexagon

    D   Octagon

©Teachers' Treasures Publishing

Name_____

DIAGNOSTIC

Common Core Standard 7.RP.A.2.C – Ratios & Proportional Relationships

☐ There are *b* bottles of juice in each of *p* packs, which makes a total of *t* bottles. Which of the following equations represents this proportional relationship? Be sure to show your work.

A $b = pt$

B $p = bt$

C $t = bp$

D $b = p + t$

Common Core Standard 7.RP.A.2.C – Ratios & Proportional Relationships

☐ There are 5 seats in each of *c* cars in the parking lot, which makes a total of *s* seats in the parking lot. Which of the following equations represents this proportional relationship? Be sure to show your work.

A $c = 5s$

B $s = 5c$

C $5 = sc$

D $s = c - 5$

Common Core Standard 7.RP.A.2.C – Ratios & Proportional Relationships

☐ An hour *h* has 60 minutes *m*. Which of the following equations represents this proportional relationship? Be sure to show your work.

A $m = 60h$

B $h = 60m$

C $60 = mh$

D $h = 60/m$

Common Core Standard 7.RP.A.2.C – Ratios & Proportional Relationships

A yard y has 3 feet f. Which of the following equations represents this proportional relationship? Be sure to show your work.

- A $y = 3 + f$
- B $y = f - 3$
- C $y = 3f$
- D $f = 3y$

Common Core Standard 7.RP.A.2.C – Ratios & Proportional Relationships

A paw p of an animal has c claws. The total number of claws is n. Which of the following equations represents this proportional relationship? Be sure to show your work.

- A $p = cn$
- B $c = np$
- C $n = pc$
- D $1 = npc$

Common Core Standard 7.RP.A.2.C – Ratios & Proportional Relationships

The total number of wheels in the garage is k. Each truck t in the garage has w wheels. Which of the following equations represents this proportional relationship? Be sure to show your work.

- A $k = tw$
- B $k = t + w$
- C $k = t - w$
- D $k = t/w$

Name_____

PRACTICE

Common Core Standard 7.RP.A.2.C – Ratios & Proportional Relationships

☐ A man walks m miles in h hours at s speed. Which of the following equations represents this proportional relationship? Be sure to show your work.

A $m = hs$

B $h = ms$

C $s = mh$

D $1 = 1/mhs$

Common Core Standard 7.RP.A.2.C – Ratios & Proportional Relationships

☐ The dimensions of a rectangular court are w and l, and its area is A. Which of the following equations represents this proportional relationship? Be sure to show your work.

A $w = Al$

B $l = Aw$

C $A = lw$

D $A = l + w$

Common Core Standard 7.RP.A.2.C – Ratios & Proportional Relationships

☐ The seats in the movie theater are arranged in r rows, with c seats in each row. The total number of seats in the movie theater is s. Which of the following equations represents this proportional relationship? Be sure to show your work.

A $s = r + c$

B $s = r - c$

C $s = r/c$

D $s = rc$

©Teachers' Treasures Publishing

Name_____

PRACTICE

Common Core Standard 7.RP.A.2.C – Ratios & Proportional Relationships

☐ There are *c* cards in *d* decks of 52 cards. Which of the following equations represents this proportional relationship? Be sure to show your work.

A $c = 52d$

B $52 = cd$

C $d = 52c$

D $52 = c + d$

Common Core Standard 7.RP.A.2.C – Ratios & Proportional Relationships

☐ The hotel has *n* beds. Each of *r* rooms has *b* beds. Which of the following equations represents this proportional relationship? Be sure to show your work.

A $n = r + b$

B $n = r - b$

C $n = r/b$

D $n = rb$

Common Core Standard 7.RP.A.2.C – Ratios & Proportional Relationships

☐ There are *k* chairs in the restaurant. There are *c* chairs around each of *t* tables. Which of the following equations represents this proportional relationship? Be sure to show your work.

A $k = c + t$

B $k = ct$

C $c = kt$

D $t = kc$

©Teachers' Treasures Publishing

Name_____

PRACTICE

Common Core Standard 7.RP.A.2.C – Ratios & Proportional Relationships

☐ There are *b* birds in the zoo. The total number of their wings is *w*. Which of the following equations represents this proportional relationship? Be sure to show your work.

    A $b = w$

    B $b = 2w$

    C $w = 2b$

    D $3w = 4b$

Common Core Standard 7.RP.A.2.C – Ratios & Proportional Relationships

☐ There are *h* hands on the photo. The number of fingers on the photo is *f*. Which of the following equations represents this proportional relationship? Be sure to show your work.

    A $h = 5f$

    B $h = 10f$

    C $f = 5h$

    D $f = 10h$

Common Core Standard 7.RP.A.2.C – Ratios & Proportional Relationships

☐ A box of chewing gum contains *c* chewing gum sticks. The number of chewing gum sticks in *p* boxes is *n*. Which of the following equations represents this proportional relationship? Be sure to show your work.

    A $c = pn$

    B $p = nc$

    C $n = pc$

    D $100 = npc$

Name_____

PRACTICE

Common Core Standard 7.RP.A.2.C – Ratios & Proportional Relationships

☐ The number of players at the basketball tournament is *p*. Each of *t* teams has 5 players. Which of the following equations represents this proportional relationship? Be sure to show your work.

A $p = 5 + t$

B $p = t/5$

C $p = t - 5$

D $p = 5t$

Common Core Standard 7.RP.A.2.C – Ratios & Proportional Relationships

☐ Alex spent *d* days in France, which is equal to *w* weeks. Which of the following equations represents this proportional relationship? Be sure to show your work.

A $w = 7d$

B $d = 7w$

C $w = d + 7$

D $d = w + 7$

Common Core Standard 7.RP.A.2.C – Ratios & Proportional Relationships

☐ Samantha is *m* months older than her brother, which is equal to *y* years. Which of the following equations represents this proportional relationship? Be sure to show your work.

A $m = 12/y$

B $y = m/12$

C $m = 12y$

D $y = 12m$

Name_____

ASSESSMENT

Common Core Standard 7.RP.A.2.C – Ratios & Proportional Relationships

☐ There are n tables in the school, arranged in c classrooms with t tables in each classroom. Which of the following equations represents this proportional relationship? Be sure to show your work.

    A $n = tc$

    B $c = nt$

    C $t = nc$

    D $100 = ntc$

Common Core Standard 7.RP.A.2.C – Ratios & Proportional Relationships

☐ Karen bought t eggs in the market arranged in p packs. Each pack contains e eggs. Which of the following equations represents this proportional relationship? Be sure to show your work.

    A $t = p + e$

    B $t = p - e$

    C $t = pe$

    D $t = p/e$

Common Core Standard 7.RP.A.2.C – Ratios & Proportional Relationships

☐ Dean earned 300 dollars working in the factory for d days. Each day he earned x dollars. Which of the following equations represents this proportional relationship? Be sure to show your work.

    A $300 = d + x$

    B $300 = dx$

    C $d = 300x$

    D $x = 300d$

©Teachers' Treasures Publishing

Name_____

ASSESSMENT

Common Core Standard 7.RP.A.2.C – Ratios & Proportional Relationships

☐ There are *p* polygons in the plane, and each polygon has *n* sides. The total number of sides of the polygons in the plane is *s*. Which of the following equations represents this proportional relationship? Be sure to show your work.

A $p = n + s$

B $p = ns$

C $n = sp$

D $s = np$

Common Core Standard 7.RP.A.2.C – Ratios & Proportional Relationships

☐ Mayda paid *s* dollars for *k* shirts. The price of each shirt is *m* dollars. Which of the following equations represents this proportional relationship? Be sure to show your work.

A $s = k + m$

B $s = k - m$

C $s = km$

D $s = k/m$

Common Core Standard 7.RP.A.2.C – Ratios & Proportional Relationships

☐ There are *p* passengers in each of *b* buses. The total number of passengers is *t*. Which of the following equations represents this proportional relationship? Be sure to show your work.

A $p = bt$

B $p = b/t$

C $t = pb$

D $t = p/b$

©Teachers' Treasures Publishing

Common Core Standard 7.RP.A.2.D – Ratios & Proportional Relationships

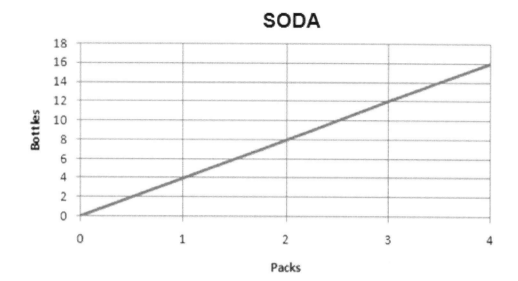

☐ Look at the graph above. Which point shows the number of bottles in a pack?

A   (0,0)   C   (2,8)

B   (1,4)   D   (4,16)

Common Core Standard 7.RP.A.2.D – Ratios & Proportional Relationships

☐ Which point must lie on the line so we can say that the line represents directly proportional relationship?

A   (0,0)   C   (2,8)

B   (1,4)   D   (4,16)

Common Core Standard 7.RP.A.2.D – Ratios & Proportional Relationships

☐ Which point shows that 3 packs contain 12 bottles of soda?

A   (3,3)   C   (3,12)

B   (12,12)   D   (12,3)

Common Core Standard 7.RP.A.2.D – Ratios & Proportional Relationships

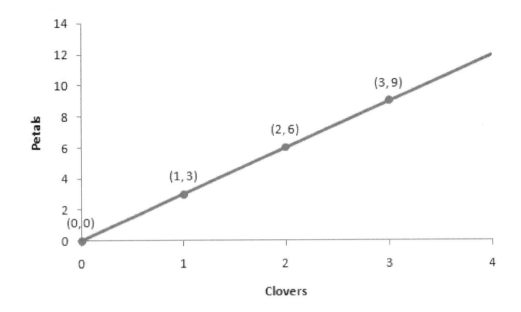

☐ Look at the graph above. Which point shows the number of petals of a clover?

A   (0,0)   C   (2,6)

B   (1,3)   D   (3,9)

Common Core Standard 7.RP.A.2.D – Ratios & Proportional Relationships

☐ Which point must lie on the line so we can say that the line represents directly proportional relationship?

A   (3,9)   C   (1,3)

B   (2,6)   D   (0,0)

Common Core Standard 7.RP.A.2.D – Ratios & Proportional Relationships

☐ Which point shows that 2 clovers have 6 petals?

A   (2,6)   C   (2,2)

B   (6,2)   D   (6,6)

Common Core Standard 7.RP.A.2.D – Ratios & Proportional Relationships

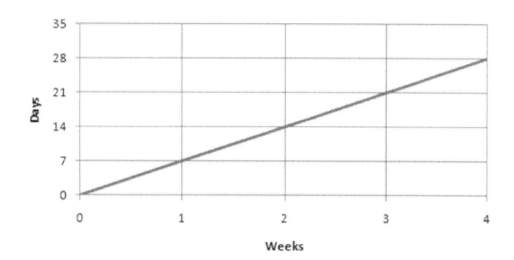

☐ Look at the graph above. Which point shows the number of days in a week?

A   (1,7)   C   (3,21)

B   (0,0)   D   (4,28)

Common Core Standard 7.RP.A.2.D – Ratios & Proportional Relationships

☐ Which point must lie on the line so we can say that the line represents directly proportional relationship?

A   (1,7)   C   (3,21)

B   (0,0)   D   (4,28)

Common Core Standard 7.RP.A.2.D – Ratios & Proportional Relationships

☐ Which point shows that 4 weeks are equal to 28 days?

A   (28,28)   C   (28,4)

B   (4,4)   D   (4,28)

Common Core Standard 7.RP.A.2.D – Ratios & Proportional Relationships

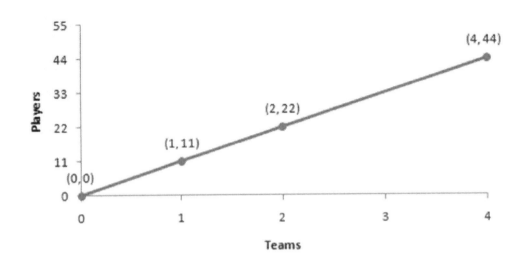

☐ Look at the graph above. Which point shows the number of players in a team?

A   (4,44)   C   (1,11)

B   (0,0)   D   (2,22)

Common Core Standard 7.RP.A.2.D – Ratios & Proportional Relationships

☐ Which point must lie on the line so we can say that the line represents directly proportional relationship?

A   (1,11)   C   (0,0)

B   (2,22)   D   (4,44)

Common Core Standard 7.RP.A.2.D – Ratios & Proportional Relationships

☐ Which point shows that 2 teams have 22 players?

A   (1,11)   C   (0,0)

B   (4,44)   D   (2,22)

Common Core Standard 7.RP.A.2.D – Ratios & Proportional Relationships

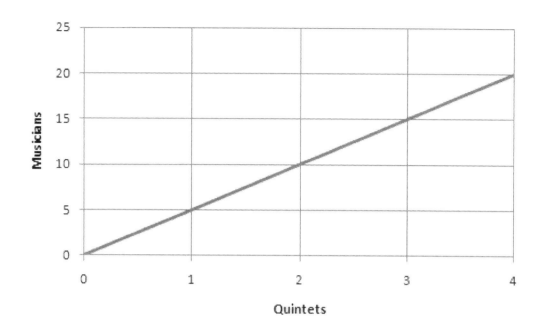

☐ Look at the graph above. How many musicians are there in a quintet?

A   5   C   15

B   10   D   20

Common Core Standard 7.RP.A.2.D – Ratios & Proportional Relationships

☐ Which point must lie on the line so we can say that the line represents directly proportional relationship?

A   (1,5)   C   (3,15)

B   (0,0)   D   (2,10)

Common Core Standard 7.RP.A.2.D – Ratios & Proportional Relationships

☐ How many quintets can be formed of 15 musicians?

A   1   C   3

B   2   D   4

Name_____

PRACTICE

Common Core Standard 7.RP.A.2.D – Ratios & Proportional Relationships

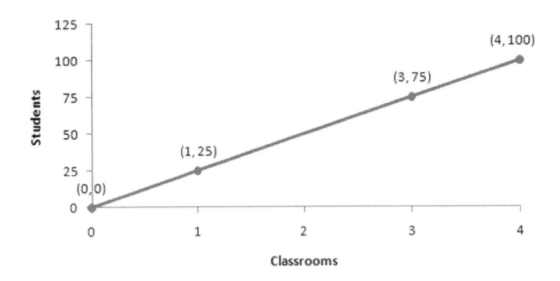

☐ Look at the graph above. How many students are there in a classroom?

A   0   C   75

B   25   D   100

Common Core Standard 7.RP.A.2.D – Ratios & Proportional Relationships

☐ Which point must lie on the line so we can say that the line represents directly proportional relationship?

A   (0,0)   C   (3,75)

B   (1,25)   D   (4,100)

Common Core Standard 7.RP.A.2.D – Ratios & Proportional Relationships

☐ How many students are there in 4 classrooms?

A   25   C   75

B   50   D   100

Common Core Standard 7.RP.A.2.D – Ratios & Proportional Relationships

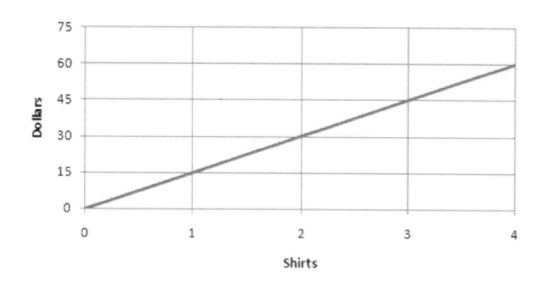

☐ Look at the graph above. How much does a shirt cost?

A $15   C $45

B $30   D $60

Common Core Standard 7.RP.A.2.D – Ratios & Proportional Relationships

☐ Which point must lie on the line so we can say that the line represents directly proportional relationship?

A   (1,15)   C   (0,0)

B   (3,45)   D   (2,30)

Common Core Standard 7.RP.A.2.D – Ratios & Proportional Relationships

☐ How many shirts can be bought for $60?

A   1   C   3

B   2   D   4

Name_____

Common Core Standard 7.RP.A.2.D – Ratios & Proportional Relationships

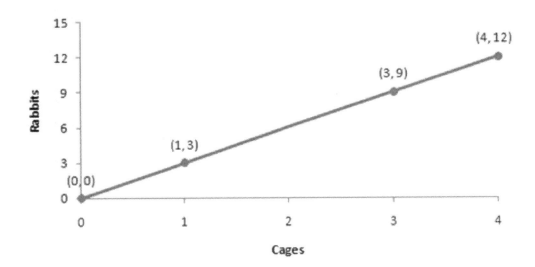

☐ Look at the graph above. How many rabbits are in a cage?

A   1   C   3

B   2   D   4

Common Core Standard 7.RP.A.2.D – Ratios & Proportional Relationships

☐ Which point must lie on the line so we can say that the line represents directly proportional relationship?

A   (1,3)   C   (0,0)

B   (3,9)   D   (4,12)

Common Core Standard 7.RP.A.2.D – Ratios & Proportional Relationships

☐ How many cages have 9 rabbits?

A   1   C   3

B   2   D   4

Name_____

DIAGNOSTIC

Common Core Standard 7.RP.A.3 – Ratios & Proportional Relationships

☐ There are 120 students in the 7th grade, and 40% of them are boys. How many boys are there in the 7th grade? Be sure to show your work.

A   40

B   48

C   60

D   72

Common Core Standard 7.RP.A.3 – Ratios & Proportional Relationships

☐ Calculate 25% of 72 and mark the correct answer below. Be sure to show your work.

A   18

B   20

C   23

D   25

Common Core Standard 7.RP.A.3 – Ratios & Proportional Relationships

☐ 8 kg of apples costs $20. How much do 6 kg of apples cost? Be sure to show your work.

A $10

B $12

C $15

D $18

©Teachers' Treasures Publishing

Name_____

DIAGNOSTIC

Common Core Standard 7.RP.A.3 – Ratios & Proportional Relationships

☐ **Jeremiah is 6 feet tall. How many inches tall is Jeremiah? Be sure to show your work.**

    A   24

    B   36

    C   48

    D   72

Common Core Standard 7.RP.A.3 – Ratios & Proportional Relationships

☐ **What is the percent of change from 30 to 21? Be sure to show your work.**

    A   30% increase

    B   30% decrease

    C   70% increase

    D   70% decrease

Common Core Standard 7.RP.A.3 – Ratios & Proportional Relationships

☐ **6 workers finish a project in 16 days. How many days do 4 workers need to finish the same project? Be sure to show your work.**

    A   18

    B   20

    C   22

    D   24

Name_____

PRACTICE

Common Core Standard 7.RP.A.3 – Ratios & Proportional Relationships

☐ Heidy buys shirts for $20 and resells for $24. What is the percentage of Heidy's mark up? Be sure to show your work.

A 4%

B 5%

C 20%

D 25%

Common Core Standard 7.RP.A.3 – Ratios & Proportional Relationships

☐ Solve for x and mark the correct answer below. Be sure to show your work.

$$12 : x = 8 : 6$$

A 8

B 9

C 10

D 11

Common Core Standard 7.RP.A.3 – Ratios & Proportional Relationships

☐ A set of dishes is marked down 30% off the original price and the sale price is $19.60. What was the original price? Be sure to show your work.

A $8.40

B $11.20

C $28

D $30

©Teachers' Treasures Publishing

Name_____

PRACTICE

Common Core Standard 7.RP.A.3 – Ratios & Proportional Relationships

☐ 3 out of 5 students in the school are boys. The total number of students is 540. How many boys are there in the school? Be sure to show your work.

- A   108
- B   216
- C   324
- D   432

Common Core Standard 7.RP.A.3 – Ratios & Proportional Relationships

☐ If x:y = 2:3 and z:y = 5:3, what is x:y:z? Be sure to show your work.

- A   2:3:5
- B   2:5:3
- C   3:5:2
- D   5:3:2

Common Core Standard 7.RP.A.3 – Ratios & Proportional Relationships

☐ Sonia put $200 in a bank that pays 8% interest per year. How much money will Sonia have in her bank account after 1 year? Be sure to show your work.

- A $184
- B $192
- C $208
- D $216

Name_____

PRACTICE

Common Core Standard 7.RP.A.3 – Ratios & Proportional Relationships

☐ There are 240 employees in the company, of which 15% are women. How many men are there in the company? Be sure to show your work.

A 15

B 36

C 204

D 225

Common Core Standard 7.RP.A.3 – Ratios & Proportional Relationships

☐ Calculate 135% of 300 and mark the correct answer below. Be sure to show your work.

A 195

B 265

C 405

D 435

Common Core Standard 7.RP.A.3 – Ratios & Proportional Relationships

☐ 3 bottles contain 4.5 liters of juice. How many liters of juice do 5 bottles contain? Be sure to show your work.

A 6.5 liters

B 7.5 liters

C 8.5 liters

D 9.5 liters

©Teachers' Treasures Publishing

Name_____

PRACTICE

Common Core Standard 7.RP.A.3 – Ratios & Proportional Relationships

☐   3 quarts of coffee cost $12.84. What is the price per cup? Be sure to show your work.

A $1.07

B $1.08

C $1.24

D $1.27

Common Core Standard 7.RP.A.3 – Ratios & Proportional Relationships

☐   What is the percent of change from 44 to 55?   Be sure to show your work.

A   11% increase

B   11% decrease

C   25% increase

D   25% decrease

Common Core Standard 7.RP.A.3 – Ratios & Proportional Relationships

☐   Jaiden travels from home to the nearest city for 3 hours at the constant speed of 60 mi/h. How many hours will Jaiden travel from home to the nearest city at the constant speed of 45 m/h? Be sure to show your work.

A   2 h

B   2.5 h

C   3.5 h

D   4 h

©Teachers' Treasures Publishing

Name_____

ASSESSMENT

Common Core Standard 7.RP.A.3 – Ratios & Proportional Relationships

☐ The car priced originally at $4,000 is on sale for $3,800. What is the percentage of the mark down? Be sure to show your work.

    A   4%

    B   5%

    C   10%

    D   20%

Common Core Standard 7.RP.A.3 – Ratios & Proportional Relationships

☐ Solve for x and mark the correct answer below. Be sure to show your work.

$$20 : 12 = x : 9$$

    A   9

    B   12

    C   15

    D   20

Common Core Standard 7.RP.A.3 – Ratios & Proportional Relationships

☐ The retail price of shoes is marked up by 20% and now the selling price is $96. What was the wholesale price? Be sure to show your work.

    A $76

    B $80

    C $84

    D $88

Name_____

ASSESSMENT

Common Core Standard 7.RP.A.3 – Ratios & Proportional Relationships

☐ **For every 2 roses in a bouquet the florist arranges 3 tulips. The total number of roses and tulips in all bouquets is 240. How many tulips are there in all bouquets? Be sure to show your work.**

A   96

B   144

C   160

D   180

Common Core Standard 7.RP.A.3 – Ratios & Proportional Relationships

☐ **If x:y = 2:3 and y:z = 6:5, what is x:y:z? Be sure to show your work.**

A   2:3:5

B   2:3:6

C   4:5:6

D   4:6:5

Common Core Standard 7.RP.A.3 – Ratios & Proportional Relationships

☐ **Arianna put $100 in a bank that pays 10% compounded annually. How much money will Arianna have in her bank account after 2 years? Be sure to show your work.**

A $110

B $115

C $120

D $121

Name_____

DIAGNOSTIC

Common Core Standard 7.NS.A.1.A – The Number System

☐ The balance on Peter's bank statement is -$20. How much money does Peter have to deposit so that the balance on his statement is $0? Be sure to show your work.

  A $0

  B $2

  C $20

  D   -$20

Common Core Standard 7.NS.A.1.A – The Number System

☐ What is the opposite number of 8? Be sure to show your work.

  A   8

  B   -8

  C   0

  D   1

Common Core Standard 7.NS.A.1.A – The Number System

☐ The temperature of the air in the afternoon was 4°C, and in the evening 0°C. What was the temperature change? Be sure to show your work.

  A   0°C

  B   2°C

  C   -2°C

  D   -4°C

©Teachers' Treasures Publishing

Name_____

DIAGNOSTIC

Common Core Standard 7.NS.A.1.A – The Number System

☐ **Michael's video game score was 250 points. After a couple of mistakes, he marked -250 points. What is Michael's overall score now? Be sure to show your work.**

A   -500

B   500

C   0

D   250

Common Core Standard 7.NS.A.1.A – The Number System

☐ **What is the opposite number of -6? Be sure to show your work.**

A   6

B   -6

C   9

D   -9

Common Core Standard 7.NS.A.1.A – The Number System

☐ **The altitude of a bird is 60 ft and the altitude of a fish in the sea is -60 ft. Which altitude is equidistant from the altitudes of a bird and a fish? Be sure to show your work.**

A   0 ft

B   -120 ft

C   120 ft

D   1 ft

©Teachers' Treasures Publishing

Name_____

PRACTICE

Common Core Standard 7.NS.A.1.A – The Number System

Element	Nitrogen	Oxygen	Fluorine	Neon	Sodium	Magnesium	Aluminum
Charge	-3	-2	-1	0	1	2	3

☐ Look at the table above. Which element should be combined with Fluorine to get 0 charge? Be sure to show your work.

A   Oxygen

B   Neon

C   Sodium

D   Magnesium

Common Core Standard 7.NS.A.1.A – The Number System

☐ Which element should be combined with Magnesium to get 0 charge? Be sure to show your work.

A   Nitrogen

B   Oxygen

C   Fluorine

D   Neon

Common Core Standard 7.NS.A.1.A – The Number System

☐ How many atoms of Sodium should be combined with Oxygen to get 0 charge? Be sure to show your work.

A   2

B   3

C   0

D   1

©Teachers' Treasures Publishing

Name_____

PRACTICE

Common Core Standard 7.NS.A.1.A – The Number System

☐ Look at the number line with story characters above. Which character is at the opposite position of the dog?

    A   Pig

    B   Tiger

    C   Cow

    D   Lion

Common Core Standard 7.NS.A.1.A – The Number System

☐ Which character is at the opposite position of the lion? Be sure to show your work.

    A   Pig

    B   Dog

    C   Tiger

    D   Cow

Common Core Standard 7.NS.A.1.A – The Number System

☐ Which character is at the opposite position to itself? Be sure to show your work.

    A   Dog

    B   Cow

    C   Pig

    D   Tiger

©Teachers' Treasures Publishing

Name_____

PRACTICE

Common Core Standard 7.NS.A.1.A – The Number System

☐ The balance on Shane's bank account is $80. Select the best answer from the below to show the figure that will bring Shane's account to $0. Be sure to show your work.

    A   -$80

    B $0

    C $80

    D   -$8

Common Core Standard 7.NS.A.1.A – The Number System

☐ What is the opposite number of -(-6)?

    A   -6

    B   6

    C   0

    D   -1

Common Core Standard 7.NS.A.1.A – The Number System

☐ The temperature of the air in the morning was $-5°C$, and in the evening $0°C$. What was the temperature change? Be sure to show your work.

    A $0°C$

    B $-5°C$

    C $5°C$

    D $10°C$

Name_____

PRACTICE

Common Core Standard 7.NS.A.1.A – The Number System

☐ **Sabrina played a video game and her score was -30 points. After a couple of good moves she scored 30 points. What is her score now? Be sure to show your work.**

    A   -60

    B   0

    C   60

    D   120

Common Core Standard 7.NS.A.1.A – The Number System

☐ **What is the opposite number of –(9)?**

    A   6

    B   -6

    C   9

    D   -9

Common Core Standard 7.NS.A.1.A – The Number System

☐ **The altitude of a plane is 1,600 ft. What must be the altitude of a submarine so that the sum of their altitudes is 0? Be sure to show your work.**

    A   0 ft

    B   -1,600 ft

    C   1,600 ft

    D   -0061 ft

©Teachers' Treasures Publishing

Name_____

ASSESSMENT

Common Core Standard 7.NS.A.1.A – The Number System

Element	Nitrogen	Oxygen	Chlorine	Argon	Potassium	Calcium	Scandium
Charge	-3	-2	-1	0	1	2	3

☐ Look at the table above. Which element should be combined with itself to get 0 charge? Be sure to show your work.

    A   Nitrogen

    B   Argon

    C   Chlorine

    D   Potassium

Common Core Standard 7.NS.A.1.A – The Number System

☐ Which element should be combined with 3 atoms of Chlorine to get 0 charge? Be sure to show your work.

    A   Nitrogen

    B   Argon

    C   Potassium

    D   Scandium

Common Core Standard 7.NS.A.1.A – The Number System

☐ How many atoms of Calcium should be combined with 2 atoms of Nitrogen to get 0 charge? Be sure to show your work.

    A   0

    B   1

    C   2

    D   3

©Teachers' Treasures Publishing

Name_____

ASSESSMENT

Common Core Standard 7.NS.A.1.A – The Number System

☐ Look at the number line above. Which vehicle is at the opposite position of the airplane? Be sure to show your work.

A   Bicycle

B   Truck

C   Bus

D   Car

Common Core Standard 7.NS.A.1.A – The Number System

☐ Which vehicle is at the opposite position of the truck? Be sure to show your work.

A   Bus

B   Car

C   Airplane

D   None of the above

Common Core Standard 7.NS.A.1.A – The Number System

☐ Which vehicle is at the opposite position of itself? Be sure to show your work.

A   Truck

B   Bus

C   Car

D   Airplane

Name_____

DIAGNOSTIC

Common Core Standard 7.NS.A.1.B – The Number System

☐ **Amanda bought a pen and an eraser. The price of the pen was $3.20 and the price of the eraser $0.90. How much did Amanda pay? Be sure to show your work.**

    A $3.10

    B $3.70

    C $4.10

    D $4.70

Common Core Standard 7.NS.A.1.B – The Number System

☐ **Look at the number line below. What is the value of P+3? Be sure to show your work.**

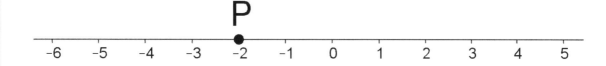

    A   -5

    B   -3

    C   -1

    D   1

Common Core Standard 7.NS.A.1.B – The Number System

☐ **The temperature of the air in the afternoon was 2°C, and in the evening -2°C. What was the temperature change? Be sure to show your work.**

    A   0°C

    B   2°C

    C   -4°C

    D   4°C

Name_____

DIAGNOSTIC

Common Core Standard 7.NS.A.1.B – The Number System

☐ **David is 1.85 m tall. His hat is 0.3 m high. How tall is David with the hat on his head? Be sure to show your work.**

- A 1.88 m
- B 1.98 m
- C 2.05 m
- D 2.15 m

Common Core Standard 7.NS.A.1.B – The Number System

☐ **Look at the number line below. What is the value of P+(-4)? Be sure to show your work.**

P is at -1 on a number line from -6 to 5.

- A -5
- B -4
- C -3
- D 3

Common Core Standard 7.NS.A.1.B – The Number System

☐ **The balance on Peter's bank statement is $40, and the balance on Olivia's bank statement is -$40. How much money would they have together? Be sure to show your work.**

- A -$80
- B $0
- C $40
- D $80

©Teachers' Treasures Publishing

Name_____

PRACTICE

Common Core Standard 7.NS.A.1.B – The Number System

☐ The dog weighs 12.6 kg and the cat weighs 9.8 kg. How much do they weigh together? Be sure to show your work.

- A 21.14 kg
- B 21.4 kg
- C 22.14 kg
- D 22.4 kg

Common Core Standard 7.NS.A.1.B – The Number System

☐ Look at the number line below. If P+x=0, what is the value of x? Be sure to show your work.

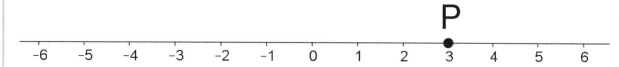

- A 0
- B 3
- C -3
- D -1

Common Core Standard 7.NS.A.1.B – The Number System

☐ The charge of the combination of atoms of Oxygen and Magnesium is 0. If the charge of Oxygen atom is +2, what is the charge of Magnesium atom? Be sure to show your work.

- A -2
- B -1
- C 0
- D 2

©Teachers' Treasures Publishing

Name_____

PRACTICE

Common Core Standard 7.NS.A.1.B – The Number System

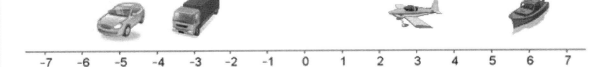

☐ The number line above shows the bank account balances for each commerical business in thousands of dollars. Which 2 businesses together have $0? Be sure to show your work.

    A   Car and airline

    B   Truck and airline

    C   Truck and ship

    D   Car and ship

Common Core Standard 7.NS.A.1.B – The Number System

☐ If the truck business earns $8,000, what will be the balance in that bank account? Be sure to show your work.

    A   -$11,000

    B   -$5,000

    C $5,000

    D $11,000

Common Core Standard 7.NS.A.1.B – The Number System

☐ If the ship withdraws $8,000, what will be the balance in that bank account? Be sure to show your work.

    A   -$14,000

    B   -$2,000

    C $2,000

    D $14,000

©Teachers' Treasures Publishing

Name_____

PRACTICE

Common Core Standard 7.NS.A.1.B – The Number System

☐ **Armand sold a shirt for $12.80 and shoes for $25.40. How much money did he earn? Be sure to show your work.**

    A $37.20

    B $37.40

    C $38.20

    D $38.40

Common Core Standard 7.NS.A.1.B – The Number System

☐ **Look at the number line below. What is the value of P+1? Be sure to show your work.**

    A   -3

    B   -1

    C   1

    D   3

Common Core Standard 7.NS.A.1.B – The Number System

☐ **The temperature of the air in the morning was -4°C, and in the afternoon 0°C. What was the temperature change? Be sure to show your work.**

    A   -8°C

    B   -4°C

    C   0°C

    D   4°C

Name_____

PRACTICE

Common Core Standard 7.NS.A.1.B – The Number System

☐ Ryan walked 1.4 miles from his home to the library and 0.75 miles from the library to the post office. What was the distance that Ryan walked? Be sure to show your work.

    A   1.115 mi

    B   1.79 mi

    C   2.115 mi

    D   2.15 mi

Common Core Standard 7.NS.A.1.B – The Number System

☐ Look at the number line below. What is the value of P+(-2)? Be sure to show your work.

    A   -7

    B   -3

    C   3

    D   7

Common Core Standard 7.NS.A.1.B – The Number System

☐ Brianna has 2 bank accounts with -$60 and $60 balance on each. How much money does Brianna have on both accounts? Be sure to show your work.

    A   -$120

    B $0

    C $60

    D $120

©Teachers' Treasures Publishing

Name _____

ASSESSMENT

Common Core Standard 7.NS.A.1.B – The Number System

☐   **On her last doctor's visit Natalie weighed 63.4 kg. On her next visit she gained 5.7 kg. How much does she weigh now?**

   A   68.1 kg

   B   68.3 kg

   C   69.1 kg

   D   69.3 kg

Common Core Standard 7.NS.A.1.B – The Number System

☐   **Look at the number line below. If P+x=0, what is the value of x? Be sure to show your work.**

```
                    P
                    ●
 -8  -7  -6  -5  -4  -3  -2  -1   0   1   2   3   4
```

   A   -8

   B   -4

   C   0

   D   4

Common Core Standard 7.NS.A.1.B – The Number System

☐   **The charge of the atom of Nitrogen is -3 and the charge of the atom of Aluminum is +3. What is the charge of their combination? Be sure to show your work.**

   A   -33

   B   -6

   C   0

   D   6

©Teachers' Treasures Publishing

Name_____

ASSESSMENT

Common Core Standard 7.NS.A.1.B – The Number System

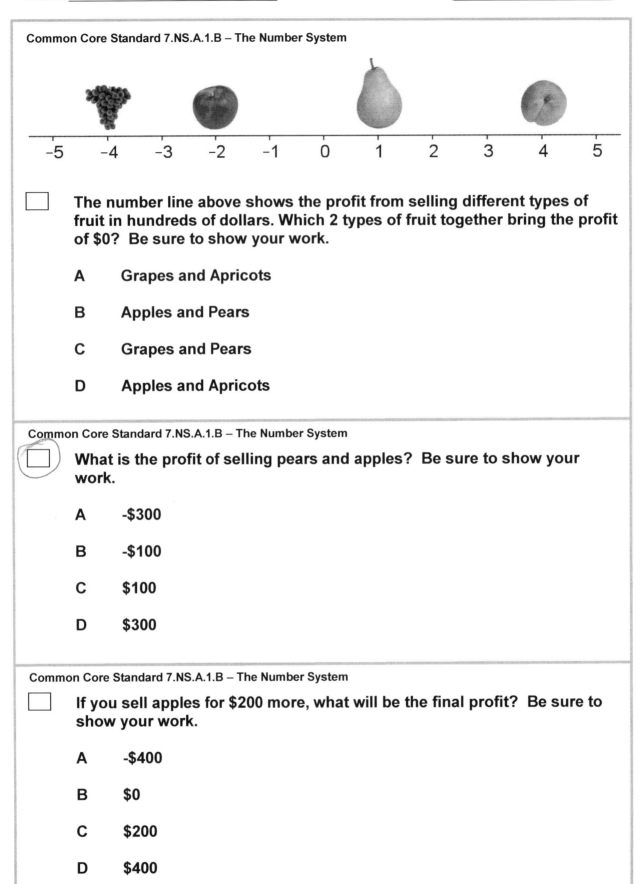

☐ The number line above shows the profit from selling different types of fruit in hundreds of dollars. Which 2 types of fruit together bring the profit of $0? Be sure to show your work.

    A   Grapes and Apricots

    B   Apples and Pears

    C   Grapes and Pears

    D   Apples and Apricots

Common Core Standard 7.NS.A.1.B – The Number System

☐ What is the profit of selling pears and apples? Be sure to show your work.

    A   -$300

    B   -$100

    C $100

    D $300

Common Core Standard 7.NS.A.1.B – The Number System

☐ If you sell apples for $200 more, what will be the final profit? Be sure to show your work.

    A   -$400

    B $0

    C $200

    D $400

©Teachers' Treasures Publishing

Name_____

DIAGNOSTIC

Common Core Standard 7.NS.A.1.C – The Number System

☐ Tyler bought a ruler and a compass. The price of the ruler was $3.40 and the price of the compass was $1.80. How much more did Tyler pay for the ruler than for the compass? Be sure to show your work.

    A $2.60

    B $2.40

    C $1.60

    D $1.40

Common Core Standard 7.NS.A.1.C – The Number System

☐ Look at the number line below. What is the value of P-4? Be sure to show your work.

    A   -6

    B   -2

    C   2

    D   6

Common Core Standard 7.NS.A.1.C – The Number System

☐ The temperature of water in the afternoon was 26°C, and in the evening 20°C. What was the temperature change? Be sure to show your work.

    A   -46°C

    B   -6°C

    C   6°C

    D   46°C

Name_____

DIAGNOSTIC

Common Core Standard 7.NS.A.1.C – The Number System

☐ **Abigail is 1.83 m tall with a hat on her head. How tall is Abigail, if the height of the hat is 0.2 m? Be sure to show your work.**

A   1.61 m

B   1.63 m

C   1.79 m

D   1.81 m

Common Core Standard 7.NS.A.1.C – The Number System

☐ **Look at the number line below. What is the value of P−(−2)? Be sure to show your work.**

A   -3

B   -1

C   1

D   3

Common Core Standard 7.NS.A.1.C – The Number System

☐ **The balance on Emily's bank statement is $80, and the balance on Ava's bank statement is -$80. How much money does Ava need to get have as much money as Emily? Be sure to show your work.**

A $0

B $40

C $80

D $160

Name_____

PRACTICE

Common Core Standard 7.NS.A.1.C – The Number System

☐ A pig weighs 42.3 kg and a goose weighs 19.7 kg. How much heavier is the pig than the goose? Be sure to show your work.

A   23.6 kg

B   23.4 kg

C   22.6 kg

D   22.4 kg

Common Core Standard 7.NS.A.1.C – The Number System

☐ Look at the number line below. What is the value of P-Q? Be sure to show your work.

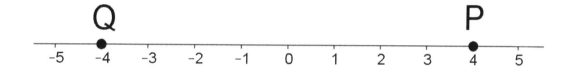

A   -8

B   -4

C   0

D   8

Common Core Standard 7.NS.A.1.C – The Number System

☐ Martin scored 120 points in a video game and Marry scored -30 points. How many more points did Martin score than Marry? Be sure to show your work.

A   150

B   90

C   -90

D   -150

Name_____

PRACTICE

Common Core Standard 7.NS.A.1.C – The Number System

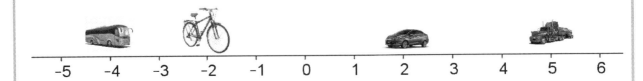

Look at the number line above. What is the distance between the bus and the truck? Be sure to show your work.

A   9

B   1

C   -1

D   -9

Common Core Standard 7.NS.A.1.C – The Number System

What is the distance between the bus and the bicycle? Be sure to show your work.

A   -4

B   -2

C   2

D   4

Common Core Standard 7.NS.A.1.C – The Number System

What is the distance between the bicycle and the car? Be sure to show your work.

A   -4

B   0

C   2

D   4

Name_____

PRACTICE

Common Core Standard 7.NS.A.1.C – The Number System

☐ **Isabella earns $12.35 per hour and Noah earns $9.50 per hour. How much more money does Isabella earn than Noah? Be sure to show your work.**

A $2.15

B $2.85

C $3.15

D $3.85

Common Core Standard 7.NS.A.1.C – The Number System

☐ **Look at the number line below. What is the value of P-3? Be sure to show your work.**

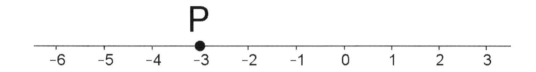

A -6

B 0

C 3

D 6

Common Core Standard 7.NS.A.1.C – The Number System

☐ **The temperature of the air in the morning was -5°C, and in the afternoon 2°C. What was the temperature change? Be sure to show your work.**

A -7°C

B -3°C

C 3°C

D 7°C

Name_____

PRACTICE

Common Core Standard 7.NS.A.1.C – The Number System

☐ **The distance from the school to the theater is 3.2 miles and the distance from the school to the post office is 1.9 miles. What is the least possible distance between the theater and the post office? Be sure to show your work.**

    A   1.3 miles

    B   1.7 miles

    C   2.3 mi

    D   2.7 mi

Common Core Standard 7.NS.A.1.C – The Number System

☐ **Look at the number line below. What is the value of P-(-1)? Be sure to show your work.**

    A   -2

    B   -1

    C   0

    D   2

Common Core Standard 7.NS.A.1.C – The Number System

☐ **Mirabai has 2 bank accounts with -$30 and $50 on each account. How much more money does Mirabai have on the 2nd account? Be sure to show your work.**

    A $20

    B $40

    C $80

    D $160

©Teachers' Treasures Publishing

Name_____

ASSESSMENT

Common Core Standard 7.NS.A.1.C – The Number System

☐ **Nicholas weighed 93.6 kg. He lost 8.9 kg. How much does he weigh now? Be sure to show your work.**

    A   84.3 kg

    B   84.7 kg

    C   85.3 kg

    D   85.7 kg

Common Core Standard 7.NS.A.1.C – The Number System

☐ **Look at the number line below. What is the distance between P and Q? Be sure to show your work.**

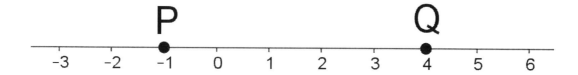

    A |-1|-|4|

    B |-1-4|

    C |4|-|-1|

    D |4-1|

Common Core Standard 7.NS.A.1.C – The Number System

☐ **The altitude of a hawk is 150 m and the altitude of a shark is -30 m. What is the shortest possible distance between the hawk and the shark? Be sure to show your work.**

    A   180 m

    B   150 m

    C   120 m

    D   30 m

©Teachers' Treasures Publishing

Name_____

ASSESSMENT

Common Core Standard 7.NS.A.1.C – The Number System

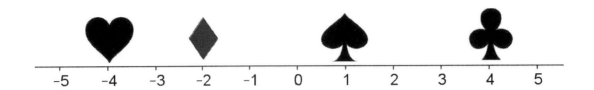

☐ Look at the number line above. What is the distance between the heart and the club? Be sure to show your work.

    A   8

    B   4

    C   2

    D   0

Common Core Standard 7.NS.A.1.C – The Number System

☐ What is the distance between the diamond and the club? Be sure to show your work.

    A   -6

    B   -2

    C   2

    D   6

Common Core Standard 7.NS.A.1.C – The Number System

☐ What is the distance between the heart and the diamond? Be sure to show your work.

    A   -6

    B   -2

    C   2

    D   6

Name_____

DIAGNOSTIC

Common Core Standard 7.NS.A.1.D – The Number System

Item	Eraser	Pencil	Ruler	Scissors
Price	$0.85	$2.49	$1.73	$5.15

☐ Look at the table above. What is the cost of a pencil and a ruler combined?

A $3.12

B $3.22

C $4.12

D $4.22

Common Core Standard 7.NS.A.1.D – The Number System

☐ How much more does a pair of scissors cost than an eraser? Be sure to show your work.

A $3.30

B $3.50

C $4.30

D $4.50

Common Core Standard 7.NS.A.1.D – The Number System

☐ How much more does a pair scissors cost than an eraser and a pencil combined? Be sure to show your work.

A $1.81

B $2.66

C $3.34

D $4.30

©Teachers' Treasures Publishing

Name_____

DIAGNOSTIC

Common Core Standard 7.NS.A.1.D – The Number System

Student	Ryan	Joseph	Taylor	Chloe
Weight (kg)	84.6	92.2	48.8	56.4

☐ Look at the table above. How much heavier is Joseph than Chloe? Be sure to show your work.

    A   35.2 kg

    B   35.8 kg

    C   36.2 kg

    D   36.8 kg

Common Core Standard 7.NS.A.1.D – The Number System

☐ What do Ryan and Taylor weigh? Be sure to show your work.

    A   132.2 kg

    B   132.4 kg

    C   133.2 kg

    D   133.4 kg

Common Core Standard 7.NS.A.1.D – The Number System

☐ How much more heavier are Taylor and Chloe than Joseph? Be sure to show your work.

    A   13 kg

    B   14 kg

    C   15 kg

    D   16 kg

Name_____

PRACTICE

Common Core Standard 7.NS.A.1.D – The Number System

Insect	June Bug	Ant	Mosquito	Butterfly
Length (cm)	2.36	1.25	3.14	5.74

☐ Look at the table above. How much longer is the mosquito compared to the ant? Be sure to show your work.

    A   1.11 cm

    B   1.89 cm

    C   2.11 cm

    D   2.89 cm

Common Core Standard 7.NS.A.1.D – The Number System

☐ How long are the June Bug and the ant combined? Be sure to show your work.

    A   3.25 cm

    B   3.36 cm

    C   3.61 cm

    D   4.61 cm

Common Core Standard 7.NS.A.1.D – The Number System

☐ How much longer is the butterfly compared to the ant and the mosquito together? Be sure to show your work.

    A   1.35 cm

    B   2.6 cm

    C   4.39 cm

    D   4.49 cm

©Teachers' Treasures Publishing

Name_____

PRACTICE

Common Core Standard 7.NS.A.1.D – The Number System

Player	Evan	Anna	Owen	Morgan
Points	23.25	18.6	28.74	20.3

☐ Look at the table above. How many more points did Owen score than Anna? Be sure to show your work.

A   10.14

B   10.62

C   10.68

D   10.8

Common Core Standard 7.NS.A.1.D – The Number System

☐ How many points did Evan and Morgan score together? Be sure to show your work.

A   43.28

B   43.35

C   43.48

D   43.55

Common Core Standard 7.NS.A.1.D – The Number System

☐ How many more points did Owen and Morgan score than Anna and Evan? Be sure to show your work.

A   7.19

B   7.46

C   8.19

D   8.46

©Teachers' Treasures Publishing

Common Core Standard 7.NS.A.1.D – The Number System

Item	Shirt	Hat	Socks	Tie
Price ($)	$12\frac{3}{4}$	$18\frac{1}{4}$	$5\frac{1}{2}$	10

☐ Look at the table above. What is the cost of the shirt and the pair of socks? Be sure to show your work.

A $17\frac{1}{4}$

B $17\frac{1}{2}$

C $18\frac{1}{4}$

D $18\frac{1}{2}$

Common Core Standard 7.NS.A.1.D – The Number System

☐ How much more does the hat cost than the pair of socks? Be sure to show your work.

A $12\frac{1}{4}$

B $12\frac{3}{4}$

C $13\frac{1}{4}$

D $13\frac{3}{4}$

Common Core Standard 7.NS.A.1.D – The Number System

☐ Which two items cost as much as the hat? Be sure to show your work.

A   Shirt and Socks

B   Socks and Tie

C   Tie and Shirt

D   None of the above

Name_____

PRACTICE

Common Core Standard 7.NS.A.1.D – The Number System

Animal	Cat	Dog	Fox	Wolf
Weight (kg)	$9\frac{2}{5}$	$11\frac{3}{4}$	$13\frac{1}{2}$	$19\frac{7}{10}$

☐ **Look at the table above. What is the weight of the cat and the fox? Be sure to show your work.**

A $22\frac{3}{10}$ kg

B $22\frac{1}{2}$ kg

C $22\frac{3}{5}$ kg

D $22\frac{9}{10}$ kg

Common Core Standard 7.NS.A.1.D – The Number System

☐ **How much heavier is the wolf than the fox? Be sure to show your work.**

A $6\frac{1}{5}$ kg

B $6\frac{1}{2}$ kg

C $6\frac{3}{4}$ kg

D $6\frac{6}{7}$ kg

Common Core Standard 7.NS.A.1.D – The Number System

☐ **How much heavier are the cat and the dog compared to the wolf? Be sure to show your work.**

A $\frac{9}{20}$ kg

B $1\frac{9}{20}$ kg

C $2\frac{9}{20}$ kg

D $3\frac{9}{20}$ kg

Name _____

ASSESSMENT

Common Core Standard 7.NS.A.1.D – The Number System

☐ **The red baton is 2.24 m long and the blue baton is 1.86 m long. How much longer is the red baton compared to the blue one? Be sure to show your work.**

    A   0.38 m

    B   0.62 m

    C   1.38 m

    D   1.62 m

Common Core Standard 7.NS.A.1.D – The Number System

☐ **Solve the problem below and mark the correct answer. Be sure to show your work.**

$$\frac{7}{8} + \frac{5}{6}$$

    A $\frac{1}{4}$

    B $\frac{6}{7}$

    C $\frac{41}{24}$

    D $\frac{41}{14}$

Common Core Standard 7.NS.A.1.D – The Number System

☐ **Alexander is 1.95 m tall and his wife is 1.67 m tall. How much taller is Alexander than his wife? Be sure to show your work.**

    A   0.22 m

    B   0.28 m

    C   0.32 m

    D   0.38

Name_____

ASSESSMENT

Common Core Standard 7.NS.A.1.D – The Number System

☐ **Serena bought $2\frac{1}{2}$ kg of apples and $3\frac{5}{8}$ kg of pears. How much fruit did she buy? Be sure to show your work.**

A $5\frac{5}{8}$ kg

B $5\frac{7}{8}$ kg

C $6\frac{1}{8}$ kg

D $6\frac{3}{8}$ kg

Common Core Standard 7.NS.A.1.D – The Number System

☐ **Solve 3.42 – 0.78 and mark the correct answer below.**

A   2.36

B   2.64

C   3.36

D   3.64

Common Core Standard 7.NS.A.1.D – The Number System

☐ **Rice ate $\frac{1}{2}$ kg of cake and $\frac{1}{4}$ kg of ice cream. How much sweets did Rice eat altogether? Be sure to show your work.**

A $\frac{1}{3}$ kg

B $\frac{3}{5}$ kg

C $\frac{3}{4}$ kg

D $\frac{5}{6}$ kg

©Teachers' Treasures Publishing

Name_____

DIAGNOSTIC

Common Core Standard 7.NS.A.2.A – The Number System

☐ **Andy bought 2.5 kg of apples priced at $3.20 per kg. How much did Andy pay for his purchase? Be sure to show your work.**

    A $5.55

    B $5.70

    C $6.40

    D $8.00

Common Core Standard 7.NS.A.2.A – The Number System

☐ **Solve the problem below and mark the correct answer. Be sure to show your work.**

$$-0.6 \times 4.3$$

    A   -2.58

    B   -1.7

    C   1.7

    D   2.58

Common Core Standard 7.NS.A.2.A – The Number System

☐ **Mason hikes at the speed of 2.1 miles per hour. How many miles will he hike in 1.5 hour? Be sure to show your work.**

    A   2.15 miles

    B   2.6 miles

    C   3.15 miles

    D   3.6 miles

©Teachers' Treasures Publishing

Name _____

DIAGNOSTIC

Common Core Standard 7.NS.A.2.A – The Number System

☐ Tyler is 6.5 feet tall. What is the best estimate of his height in meters? (Note: 1 ft ≈ 0.3 m) Be sure to show your work.

- A   1.65 m
- B   1.75 m
- C   1.85 m
- D   1.95 m

Common Core Standard 7.NS.A.2.A – The Number System

☐ Solve the problem below and mark the correct answer. Be sure to show your work.

$$(-2.3) \times (-4.7)$$

- A   -10.81
- B   -7
- C   7
- D   10.81

Common Core Standard 7.NS.A.2.A – The Number System

☐ The distance between two cities is 52.7 miles. What is the best estimate of the distance between the two cities in kilometers? (Note: 1 mi ≈ 1.6 km) Be sure to show your work.

- A   84.32 km
- B   90 km
- C   94.32 km
- D   100 km

©Teachers' Treasures Publishing

Name_____

PRACTICE

Common Core Standard 7.NS.A.2.A – The Number System

☐ **Leila weighs 144.8 lbs. What is the best estimate of her weight in kilograms? (Note: 1 lb≈0.5 kg) Be sure to show your work.**

    A   72.4 kg

    B   72.8 kg

    C   77.4 kg

    D   77.8 kg

Common Core Standard 7.NS.A.2.A – The Number System

☐ **Which expression is equivalent to the expression below? Be sure to show your work.**

$$0.4 \times (x - 1.8)$$

    A   0.4x – 1.4

    B   0.4x – 2.2

    C   0.72x

    D   0.4x – 0.72

Common Core Standard 7.NS.A.2.A – The Number System

☐ **What is the best estimate of the mass of 8.5 fluid ounces of water in kilograms? (Note: 1 fl oz≈0.03 kg) Be sure to show your work.**

    A   0.20 kg

    B   0.25 kg

    C   0.3 kg

    D   0.35 kg

Name_____

PRACTICE

Common Core Standard 7.NS.A.2.A – The Number System

☐ **What is the area of the kitchen floor, the width of which is 2.3 m and length is 3.1 m? Be sure to show your work.**

- A $5.4 \, m^2$
- B $6.3 \, m^2$
- C $7.13 \, m^2$
- D $23.31 \, m^2$

Common Core Standard 7.NS.A.2.A – The Number System

☐ **Which expression is equivalent to the expression below? Be sure to show your work.**

$$(x + 1.3) \times 0.2$$

- A 0.26x
- B 0.2x + 0.26
- C 0.2x + 1.5
- D 0.2x + 0.6

Common Core Standard 7.NS.A.2.A – The Number System

☐ **What is the area of the screen of mobile phone, the width of which is 4.2 cm and length is 7.6 cm? Be sure to show your work.**

- A $29.92 \, cm^2$
- B $30.08 \, cm^2$
- C $31.92 \, cm^2$
- D $32.08 \, cm^2$

©Teachers' Treasures Publishing

Name_____

PRACTICE

Common Core Standard 7.NS.A.2.A – The Number System

☐ **John bought 1.6 kg of sugar priced at $2.4 per kg. How much did he John pay for his purchase? Be sure to show your work.**

    A $3.16

    B $3.84

    C $4.16

    D $4.84

Common Core Standard 7.NS.A.2.A – The Number System

☐ **Solve the problem below and mark the correct answer. Be sure to show your work.**

$$5.2 \times (-2.6)$$

    A   -13.52

    B   -7.8

    C   7.8

    D   13.52

Common Core Standard 7.NS.A.2.A – The Number System

☐ **Anahit rides her bicycle at a constant speed of 4.2 miles per hour. How many miles will she pass in 2.5 hours? Be sure to show your work.**

    A   5 miles

    B   6.7 miles

    C   8 miles

    D   10.5 miles

©Teachers' Treasures Publishing

Name_____

PRACTICE

Common Core Standard 7.NS.A.2.A – The Number System

☐ **Mila's house is 5.2 yards high. What is the best estimate of the height of Mila's house in meters? (Note: 1 yd ≈ 0.9 m) Be sure to show your work.**

- A   4.3 m
- B   4.7 m
- C   5.3 m
- D   5.7 m

Common Core Standard 7.NS.A.2.A – The Number System

☐ **Solve the problem below and mark the correct answer. Be sure to show your work.**

$$7.3 \times 4.1$$

- A   -29.93
- B   -28.3
- C   28.3
- D   29.93

Common Core Standard 7.NS.A.2.A – The Number System

☐ **The length of a pencil is 7.5 inches. What is the best estimate of this length in centimeters? (Note: 1 in ≈ 2.5 cm) Be sure to show your work.**

- A   9.1 cm
- B   14.25 cm
- C   18.75 cm
- D   72.55 cm

Name_____

ASSESSMENT

Common Core Standard 7.NS.A.2.A – The Number System

☐ **Sargis weighs 168.6 lbs. What is the best estimate of his weight in kilograms? (Note: 1 lb≈0.5 kg) Be sure to show your work.**

A   84.3 kg

B   88.3 kg

C   92.3 kg

D   96.3 kg

Common Core Standard 7.NS.A.2.A – The Number System

☐ **Which expression is equivalent to the expression below? Be sure to show your work.**

$$(-1.2) \times (x + 0.5)$$

A   -0.6x

B   0.6x

C   -1.2x – 0.6

D   -1.2x + 0.6

Common Core Standard 7.NS.A.2.A – The Number System

☐ **What is the best estimate of the mass of 6.5 tablespoons of water in grams? (Note: 1 tbsp≈14.8 g) Be sure to show your work.**

A   78 g

B   84 g

C   90 g

D   96 g

©Teachers' Treasures Publishing

Name_____

ASSESSMENT

Common Core Standard 7.NS.A.2.A – The Number System

☐ **What is the area of the picture, the width of which is 1.8 m and the height is 0.8 m? Be sure to show your work.**

- A   1.44 m²
- B   1.6 m²
- C   2.6 m²
- D   2.64 m²

Common Core Standard 7.NS.A.2.A – The Number System

☐ **Which expression is equivalent to the expression below? Be sure to show your work.**

$$(0.4 - x) \times (-1.3)$$

- A   0.52x
- B   -0.52 + 1.3x
- C   0.52 – 1.3x
- D   -0.52 – 1.3x

Common Core Standard 7.NS.A.2.A – The Number System

☐ **What is the area of the photograph, the width of which is 16.4 cm and the height is 10.5 cm? Be sure to show your work.**

- A   160.2 cm²
- B   160.8 cm²
- C   172.2 cm²
- D   172.8 cm²

©Teachers' Treasures Publishing

Name _____

DIAGNOSTIC

Common Core Standard 7.NS.A.2.B – The Number System

☐ For his project, Samuel bought 6 equal pieces of wood with a total length of 5.1 m. What is the length of each piece of wood? Be sure to show your work.

    A   0.55 m

    B   0.65 m

    C   0.75 m

    D   0.85 m

Common Core Standard 7.NS.A.2.B – The Number System

☐ Solve the problem below and mark the correct answer. Be sure to show your work.

$$-11.06 \div 7$$

    A   -4.06

    B   -1.58

    C   1.58

    D   4.06

Common Core Standard 7.NS.A.2.B – The Number System

☐ 8 equal packs of ice cream weigh 6 kg. How much does one pack weigh? Be sure to show your work.

    A   0.75 kg

    B   0.68 kg

    C   0.86 kg

    D   1.33 kg

©Teachers' Treasures Publishing

Name_____

DIAGNOSTIC

Common Core Standard 7.NS.A.2.B – The Number System

☐ **The area of a rectangular playground is 84 yd². The width of the playground is 8 yd. How long is the playground? Be sure to show your work.**

A   9.5 yd

B   10.5 yd

C   11.5 yd

D   12.5 yd

Common Core Standard 7.NS.A.2.B – The Number System

☐ **Solve the problem below and mark the correct answer. Be sure to show your work.**

$$24 \div (-30)$$

A   -0.8

B   -0.6

C   0.6

D   0.8

Common Core Standard 7.NS.A.2.B – The Number System

☐ **At the airport Markus exchanged €25 into $33. What was the exchange rate at the airport? Be sure to show your work.**

A $0.76 for €1

B $0.95 for €1

C $1.14 for €1

D $1.32 for €1

©Teachers' Treasures Publishing

Name_____

PRACTICE

Common Core Standard 7.NS.A.2.B – The Number System

☐ Armenak spent 3 hours walking from his home to the nearby lake. If the distance from Armenak's home to the lake is 5.4 miles, what was his average speed? Be sure to show your work.

A   1.4 mi/h

B   1.8 mi/h

C   2.4 mi/h

D   2.8 mi/h

Common Core Standard 7.NS.A.2.B – The Number System

☐ Complete the multiplication sentence below and mark the correct answer. Be sure to show your work.

$$5 \times \underline{} = 3.75$$

A   0.65

B   0.7

C   0.75

D   0.8

Common Core Standard 7.NS.A.2.B – The Number System

☐ The distance between two cities is 80 km. What is the best estimate of the distance between the two cities in miles? (Note: 1 mi ≈ 1.6 km) Be sure to show your work.

A   40 mi

B   50 mi

C   60 mi

D   70 mi

©Teachers' Treasures Publishing

Name_____

PRACTICE

Common Core Standard 7.NS.A.2.B – The Number System

☐ **Liana weighs 65.6 kg. What is the best estimate of Liana's weight in pounds? (Note: 1 kg ≈ 0.5 lb) Be sure to show your work.**

- A   130.12 lb
- B   130.2 lb
- C   131.12 lb
- D   131.2 lb

Common Core Standard 7.NS.A.2.B – The Number System

☐ **Complete the division sentence below and mark the correct answer. Be sure to show your work.**

$$112.5 \div \_\_\_\_ = 9$$

- A   11.25
- B   11.5
- C   12.25
- D   12.5

Common Core Standard 7.NS.A.2.B – The Number System

☐ **The City Hall building is 28 m high. Each floor is 3.5 m high. How many floors does the City Hall have? Be sure to show your work.**

- A   6
- B   7
- C   8
- D   9

©Teachers' Treasures Publishing

Name _____

PRACTICE

Common Core Standard 7.NS.A.2.B – The Number System

☐ **Irene paid $14.20 for 4 kg of strawberries. What was the price of 1 kg of strawberries? Be sure to show your work.**

- A $3.45
- B $3.55
- C $3.65
- D $3.75

Common Core Standard 7.NS.A.2.B – The Number System

☐ **Solve the problem below and mark the correct answer. Be sure to show your work.**

$$(-48.48) \div (-12)$$

- A -4.4
- B -4.04
- C 4.04
- D 4.4

Common Core Standard 7.NS.A.2.B – The Number System

☐ **Hannah paid $11 for 4 m of purple ribbon. How much did 1 m of ribbon cost? Be sure to show your work.**

- A $2.25
- B $2.75
- C $3.25
- D $3.75

©Teachers' Treasures Publishing

Name_____

PRACTICE

Common Core Standard 7.NS.A.2.B – The Number System

☐ The area of a rectangular parking lot is 610 yd². The length of the parking lot is 25 yd. How wide is the parking lot? Be sure to show your work.

    A   24.4 yd

    B   24.6 yd

    C   25.4 yd

    D   25.6 yd

Common Core Standard 7.NS.A.2.B – The Number System

☐ Solve the problem below and mark the correct answer. Be sure to show your work.

$$24 \div 16$$

    A   -1.5

    B   -0.66

    C   0.66

    D   1.5

Common Core Standard 7.NS.A.2.B – The Number System

☐ For his vacation to London, Justin changed $55 into £33. What exchange rate did Justin use? Be sure to show your work.

    A   £0.6 for $1

    B   £0.9 for $1

    C   £1.34 for $1

    D   £1.67 for $1

©Teachers' Treasures Publishing

Name_____

ASSESSMENT

Common Core Standard 7.NS.A.2.B – The Number System

☐ Gibson travelled 4 hours by bus and crossed 210 miles. What was the average speed of the bus? Be sure to show your work.

A   51.5 mi/h

B   52.5 mi/h

C   53.5 mi/h

D   54.5 mi/h

Common Core Standard 7.NS.A.2.B – The Number System

☐ Complete multiplication sentence below and mark the correct answer. Be sure to show your work.

$$\_\_\_ \times (-7) = 32.55$$

A   -4.65

B   -4.35

C   4.35

D   4.65

Common Core Standard 7.NS.A.2.B – The Number System

☐ The altitude of a small plane is 3,000 ft. What is the best estimate of the altitude of the plane in centimeters? (Note: 1 cm ≈ 0.03 ft) Be sure to show your work.

A   100 cm

B   1,000 cm

C   10,000 cm

D   100,000 cm

©Teachers' Treasures Publishing

Name_____

ASSESSMENT

Common Core Standard 7.NS.A.2.B – The Number System

☐ **How many cups are in 4.5 quarts? (Note: 1 cup = 0.25 quart) Be sure to show your work.**

    A   9 cups

    B   18 cups

    C   27 cups

    D   36 cups

Common Core Standard 7.NS.A.2.B – The Number System

☐ **Complete division sentence below and mark the correct answer. Be sure to show your work.**

$$(-8) \div \underline{} = 40$$

    A   -5

    B   -0.2

    C   0.2

    D   5

Common Core Standard 7.NS.A.2.B – The Number System

☐ **The length of a tile is 32.5 cm. How many tiles are needed to cover the floor which length is 520 cm? Be sure to show your work.**

    A   16

    B   17

    C   18

    D   19

©Teachers' Treasures Publishing

Name _____

DIAGNOSTIC

Common Core Standard 7.NS.A.2.C – The Number System

☐ Use the grid to fill in the missing number below. Be sure to show your work.

0.6 x 0.2 = _____

A 0.08 m²

B 0.12 m²

C 0.32 m²

D 0.48 m²

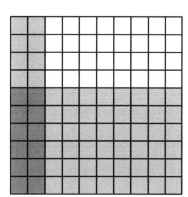

Common Core Standard 7.NS.A.2.C – The Number System

☐ Solve the problem below and mark the correct anwer. Be sure to show your work.

$$\frac{2}{5} \div \frac{8}{15}$$

A $\frac{1}{4}$

B $\frac{3}{4}$

C $\frac{4}{3}$

D $\frac{8}{3}$

Common Core Standard 7.NS.A.2.C – The Number System

☐ 8 equal packs of sugar weigh 9.6 kg. The price of sugar is $2.70 per kg. What is the price of one pack of sugar? Be sure to show your work.

A $2.24   C $3.24

B $2.76   D $3.76

Name_____

DIAGNOSTIC

Common Core Standard 7.NS.A.2.C – The Number System

☐ Use the grid to fill in the missing number below. Be sure to show your work.

$\dfrac{1}{4} \times \dfrac{2}{3} =$ _____

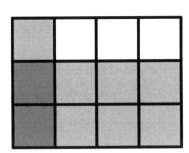

A $\dfrac{1}{12}$

B $\dfrac{2}{12}$

C $\dfrac{3}{12}$

D $\dfrac{4}{12}$

Common Core Standard 7.NS.A.2.C – The Number System

☐ Solve the problem below and mark the correct answer. Be sure to show your work.

2.6 x 1.8

A 2.48

B 3.4

C 4.4

D 4.68

Common Core Standard 7.NS.A.2.C – The Number System

☐ The seats are arranged in 8 rows with 6 seats in each row. If the seats are arranged in 12 rows, what would be the number of seats in each row? Be sure to show your work.

A 4   C 6

B 5   D 7

©Teachers' Treasures Publishing

Name_____

PRACTICE

Common Core Standard 7.NS.A.2.C – The Number System

☐ Use the grid to fill in the missing number below. Be sure to show your work.

0.5 x 0.3 = ____

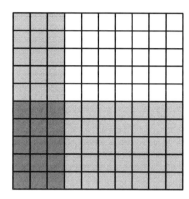

A   0.15

B   0.35

C   0.53

D   1.5

Common Core Standard 7.NS.A.2.C – The Number System

☐ Solve the problem below and mark the correct answer. Be sure to show your work.

$$2\frac{2}{3} \div 1\frac{1}{3}$$

A   2

B $2\frac{1}{3}$

C $2\frac{2}{3}$

D   3

Common Core Standard 7.NS.A.2.C – The Number System

☐ The cars on the parking lot are arranged in 9 rows with 8 cars in each row. If the cars are arranged in 24 rows, what would be the number of cars in each row? Be sure to show your work.

A   2

B   3

C   4

D   5

Name_____

PRACTICE

Common Core Standard 7.NS.A.2.C – The Number System

☐ **Use the grid to fill in the missing number below. Be sure to show your work.**

$\dfrac{2}{5} \times \dfrac{3}{4} = $ _____

A $\dfrac{2}{20}$

B $\dfrac{3}{20}$

C $\dfrac{6}{20}$

D $\dfrac{9}{20}$

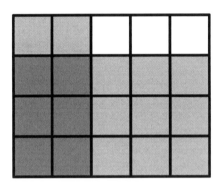

Common Core Standard 7.NS.A.2.C – The Number System

☐ **Solve the problem below and mark the correct answer. Be sure to show your work.**

0.25 x 2.8

A   0.7

B   1.3

C   1.7

D   2.3

Common Core Standard 7.NS.A.2.C – The Number System

☐ **The price of 1 liter of soda is $1.85. A pack of soda contains 6 bottles of 1.5 liter each. What is the price of a pack of soda? Be sure to show your work.**

A $15.35   C $16.35

B $15.65   D $16.65

©Teachers' Treasures Publishing

Name_____

PRACTICE

Common Core Standard 7.NS.A.2.C – The Number System

☐ **Use the grid to fill in the missing number below. Be sure to show your work.**

0.24 ÷ 0.4 = ___

A 0.16

B 0.24

C 0.36

D 0.6

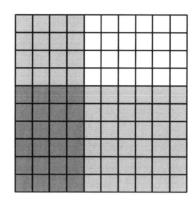

Common Core Standard 7.NS.A.2.C – The Number System

☐ **Solve the problem below and mark the correct answer. Be sure to show your work.**

$$\frac{1}{3} \div \frac{4}{9}$$

A $\frac{1}{4}$　　　　　　　　C $\frac{3}{4}$

B $\frac{4}{12}$　　　　　　　D $\frac{4}{3}$

Common Core Standard 7.NS.A.2.C – The Number System

☐ **5 equal bags of bananas weigh 4.5 kg. The price of 1 kg of bananas is $4.20. What is the price of one bag of bananas? Be sure to show your work.**

A $3.22

B $3.78

C $4.22

D $4.78

©Teachers' Treasures Publishing　　　　　　　　Page 101

Name_____

PRACTICE

Common Core Standard 7.NS.A.2.C – The Number System

☐ Use the grid to fill in the missing number below. Be sure to show your work.

$$\frac{5}{12} \div \frac{1}{2} = \underline{}$$

A $\frac{5}{6}$

B $\frac{1}{24}$

C $\frac{6}{14}$

D $\frac{4}{10}$

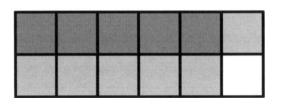

Common Core Standard 7.NS.A.2.C – The Number System

☐ Solve the problem below and mark the correct answer. Be sure to show your work.

$$0.4 \times 0.25 = \underline{}$$

A 10

B 1

C 0.1

D 0.01

Common Core Standard 7.NS.A.2.C – The Number System

☐ While moving to a new location, Lucia found 9 boxes with 4 dolls in each box. She rearranged dolls so that each box contains 6 dolls. How many boxes did she use? Be sure to show your work.

A 4

B 5

C 6

D 7

©Teachers' Treasures Publishing

Name_____

ASSESSMENT

Common Core Standard 7.NS.A.2.C – The Number System

☐ Use the grid to fill in the missing number below. Be sure to show your work.

0.28 ÷ ___ = 0.7

A   0.18

B   0.21

C   0.35

D   0.4

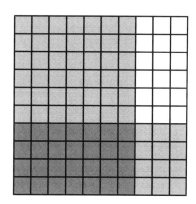

Common Core Standard 7.NS.A.2.C – The Number System

☐ Solve the problem below and mark the correct answer. Be sure to show your work.

$$4 \div 2\frac{1}{2}$$

A $2\frac{1}{2}$

B $1\frac{3}{5}$

C $1\frac{1}{2}$

D $1\frac{1}{5}$

Common Core Standard 7.NS.A.2.C – The Number System

☐ At a pet store parrots are arranged in 18 cages with 3 parrots in each cage. How many cages are needed so that only 2 parrots are in each cage? Be sure to show your work.

A   21

B   23

C   25

D   27

©Teachers' Treasures Publishing

Name_____

ASSESSMENT

Common Core Standard 7.NS.A.2.C – The Number System

☐ Use the grid to fill in the missing number below. Be sure to show your work.

$\frac{1}{6} \div \underline{} = \frac{1}{2}$

A $\frac{1}{6}$

B $\frac{2}{6}$

C $\frac{3}{6}$

D $\frac{4}{6}$

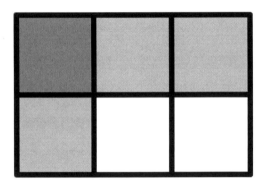

Common Core Standard 7.NS.A.2.C – The Number System

☐ Solve the problem below and mark the correct answer. Be sure to show your work.

4.4 x 0.2

A 0.22

B 0.88

C 2.2

D 8.8

Common Core Standard 7.NS.A.2.C – The Number System

☐ The price of 5 boxes of chocolates is $22. A box of chocolates contains 4 pieces. What is the price of one piece of chocolate? Be sure to show your work.

A $1.1   C $3.3

B $2.2   D $4.4

©Teachers' Treasures Publishing   Page 104

Name_____

DIAGNOSTIC

Common Core Standard 7.NS.A.2.D – The Number System

☐ The length of a regular walking stick is $\frac{3}{5}$ m. Which decimal number also represents the length of the walking stick? Be sure to show your work.

    A   0.35 m

    B   0.53 m

    C   0.6 m

    D   0.8 m

Common Core Standard 7.NS.A.2.D – The Number System

☐ Convert $\frac{3}{8}$ to a decimal number using long division. Be sure to show your work.

    A   0.375

    B   0.38

    C   0.825

    D   0.83

Common Core Standard 7.NS.A.2.D – The Number System

☐ The weight of a shipment box at a post office is $\frac{3}{4}$ kg. Which decimal number also represents the weight of the box? Be sure to show your work.

    A   0.34 kg

    B   0.43 kg

    C   0.57 kg

    D   0.75 kg

©Teachers' Treasures Publishing

Name_____

DIAGNOSTIC

Common Core Standard 7.NS.A.2.D – The Number System

☐ Abraam has $\frac{1}{4}$ of a dollar. Which decimal number also represents the amount of money that Abraam has? Be sure to show your work.

    A $0.14

    B $0.25

    C $0.41

    D $0.52

Common Core Standard 7.NS.A.2.D – The Number System

☐ Convert $\frac{1}{5}$ to a decimal number using long division. Be sure to show your work.

    A   0.15

    B   0.2

    C   0.5

    D   0.51

Common Core Standard 7.NS.A.2.D – The Number System

☐ Mara's dining table is $\frac{7}{8}$ m high. Which decimal number also represents the height of Mara's table? Be sure to show your work.

    A   0.775 m

    B   0.78 m

    C   0.87 m

    D   0.875 m

Name_____

PRACTICE

Common Core Standard 7.NS.A.2.D – The Number System

☐ A bottle contains $\frac{5}{6}$ liters of water. Which decimal number best estimates the amount of water in the bottle? Be sure to show your work.

    A   0.38 liters

    B   0.56 liters

    C   0.65 liters

    D   0.83 liters

Common Core Standard 7.NS.A.2.D – The Number System

☐ What is the repeating part of the decimal number equivalent to $\frac{4}{7}$?

    A   571

    B   5714

    C   57142

    D   571428

Common Core Standard 7.NS.A.2.D – The Number System

☐ The distance between two villages is $\frac{8}{9}$ miles. Which decimal number best estimates the distance between the two villages? Be sure to show your work.

    A   0.89 miles

    B   0.91 miles

    C   0.96 miles

    D   0.98 miles

©Teachers' Treasures Publishing

Name_____

PRACTICE

Common Core Standard 7.NS.A.2.D – The Number System

☐ Nelson is carrying a bag with $\frac{1}{2}$ kg of oranges. Which decimal number also represents the weight of Nelson's bag? Be sure to show your work.

A   0.12 kg

B   0.2 kg

C   0.21 kg

D   0.5 kg

Common Core Standard 7.NS.A.2.D – The Number System

☐ What is the repeating part of the decimal number equivalent to $\frac{2}{3}$? Be sure to show your work.

A   2

B   3

C   6

D   12

Common Core Standard 7.NS.A.2.D – The Number System

☐ The area of the school gym window is $\frac{7}{9}$ square meters. Which decimal number best estimates the area of the gym window? Be sure to show your work.

A   0.78 square meters

B   0.79 square meters

C   0.97 square meters

D   0.98 square meters

©Teachers' Treasures Publishing

Name_____

PRACTICE

Common Core Standard 7.NS.A.2.D – The Number System

☐ The width of Nara's kitchen is $3\frac{2}{5}$ m. Which decimal number also represents the length of Nara's kitchen? Be sure to show your work.

    A   3.2 m

    B   3.2 m

    C   3.25 m

    D   3.4 m

Common Core Standard 7.NS.A.2.D – The Number System

☐ Convert $1\frac{5}{8}$ to a decimal number using long division. Be sure to show your work.

    A   1.58

    B   1.625

    C   1.85

    D   1.925

Common Core Standard 7.NS.A.2.D – The Number System

☐ Bidisha bought $2\frac{1}{4}$ kg of pears. Which decimal number also represents the weight of pears that Bidisha bought? Be sure to show your work.

    A   2.1 kg

    B   2.14 kg

    C   2.25 kg

    D   2.4 kg

©Teachers' Treasures Publishing

Name_____

PRACTICE

Common Core Standard 7.NS.A.2.D – The Number System

☐ **Marietta spent $6\frac{1}{2}$ dollars on snacks. Which decimal number also represents the amount of money that Marietta spent? Be sure to show your work.**

   A $6.10

   B $6.12

   C $6.21

   D $6.50

Common Core Standard 7.NS.A.2.D – The Number System

☐ **Convert $\frac{1}{5}$ to a decimal number using long division. Be sure to show your work.**

   A   0.15

   B   0.2

   C   0.5

   D   0.51

Common Core Standard 7.NS.A.2.D – The Number System

☐ **Boris' office chair is $\frac{7}{8}$ m high. Which decimal number also represents the height of Boris' chair? Be sure to show your work.**

   A   0.775 m

   B   0.78 m

   C   0.87 m

   D   0.875 m

©Teachers' Treasures Publishing

Name_____

ASSESSMENT

Common Core Standard 7.NS.A.2.D – The Number System

☐ Anna's favorite pot contains $3\frac{3}{4}$ liters of water. Which decimal number also represents the amount of water in Anna's pot? Be sure to show your work.

    A   3.34 liters

    B   3.43 liters

    C   3.57 liters

    D   3.75 liters

Common Core Standard 7.NS.A.2.D – The Number System

☐ What is the repeating part of the decimal number equivalent to $\frac{1}{6}$? Be sure to show your work.

    A   1

    B   16

    C   6

    D   61

Common Core Standard 7.NS.A.2.D – The Number System

☐ Penelope jogged $2\frac{1}{7}$ miles. Which decimal number best estimates the distance that Penelope jogged? Be sure to show your work.

    A   2.14 miles

    B   2.17 miles

    C   2.71 miles

    D   2.74 miles

©Teachers' Treasures Publishing

Name_____

ASSESSMENT

Common Core Standard 7.NS.A.2.D – The Number System

☐ Mary is $5\frac{2}{3}$ ft tall. Which decimal number best estimates Mary's height? Be sure to show your work.

    A   5.2 ft

    B   5.23 ft

    C   5.3 ft

    D   5.67 ft

Common Core Standard 7.NS.A.2.D – The Number System

☐ What is the repeating part of the decimal number equivalent to $\frac{4}{9}$? Be sure to show your work.

    A   4

    B   9

    C   49

    D   94

Common Core Standard 7.NS.A.2.D – The Number System

☐ The area of a classroom wall is $6\frac{3}{10}$ square meters. Which decimal number also represents the area of the wall? Be sure to show your work.

    A   6.1 square meters

    B   6.13 square meters

    C   6.3 square meters

    D   6.31 square meters

©Teachers' Treasures Publishing

Name_____

DIAGNOSTIC

Common Core Standard 7.NS.A.3 – The Number System

☐ For his science fair project Jacob measured insects. The ant was 0.85 cm long, while the roach was 2.6 cm long. How many centimeters was the roach longer than the ant? Be sure to show your work.

    A   1.25 cm

    B   1.75 cm

    C   1.85 cm

    D   2.25 cm

Common Core Standard 7.NS.A.3 – The Number System

☐ What is the value of the expression below? Be sure to show your work.

$$\frac{3}{2} \times \left(2 - \frac{1}{3}\right)$$

    A $2\frac{1}{3}$

    B $2\frac{1}{2}$

    C $2\frac{2}{3}$

    D   3

Common Core Standard 7.NS.A.3 – The Number System

☐ Five friends shared equally $1\frac{1}{4}$ kg of ice cream. How much ice cream did each of them get? Be sure to show your work.

    A $\frac{1}{8}$ kg   C $\frac{1}{5}$ kg

    B $\frac{1}{6}$ kg   D $\frac{1}{4}$ kg

©Teachers' Treasures Publishing

Name_____

DIAGNOSTIC

Common Core Standard 7.NS.A.3 – The Number System

☐ The price of a workbook online was $2.35 and the price of a pencil was $1.15. Dhisha bought 2 workbooks and 3 pencils. How much did Dhisha pay without the shipping cost? Be sure to show your work.

- A $8.15
- B $8.35
- C $9.15
- D $9.35

Common Core Standard 7.NS.A.3 – The Number System

☐ What is the value of the expression below? Be sure to show your work.

$$11 \div \left(1 + \frac{5}{6}\right)$$

- A 1
- B 5
- C 6
- D 11

Common Core Standard 7.NS.A.3 – The Number System

☐ Ruby bought 3.2 lbs of bananas, 4.9 lbs of grapes, and 5.1 lbs of sugar. How much fruit did Ruby buy? Be sure to show your work.

- A 7.1 lbs
- B 7.7 lbs
- C 8.1 lbs
- D 8.7 lbs

©Teachers' Treasures Publishing

Name_____

PRACTICE

Common Core Standard 7.NS.A.3 – The Number System

☐ How many liters of juice are there in 5 six-packs and 3 four-packs, if each juice box in a pack contains 1.5 liters of liquid? Be sure to show your work.

- A 42 liters
- B 43 liters
- C 62 liters
- D 63 liters

Common Core Standard 7.NS.A.3 – The Number System

☐ What is the value of the expression below? Be sure to show your work.

$$\left(1 - \frac{1}{3}\right) \div \left(\frac{1}{3} - \frac{1}{6}\right)$$

- A -4
- B $-\frac{1}{4}$
- C $\frac{1}{4}$
- D 4

Common Core Standard 7.NS.A.3 – The Number System

☐ Aria cut a cake and served it all on 12 plates. Each plate contains 0.35 kg of cake. How much did the cake weigh? Be sure to show your work.

- A 3.2 kg
- B 4.2 kg
- C 5.2 kg
- D 6.2 kg

©Teachers' Treasures Publishing

Name_____

PRACTICE

Common Core Standard 7.NS.A.3 – The Number System

☐ **The temperature in the morning was 67.8°F, and in the afternoon it was 75.4°F. What was the temperature change? Be sure to show your work.**

    A   7.4°F

    B   7.6°F

    C   8.4°F

    D   8.6°F

Common Core Standard 7.NS.A.3 – The Number System

☐ **What is the value of the expression below? Be sure to show your work.**

$$\left(\frac{1}{3} - \frac{1}{2}\right) \times \left(1 + \frac{1}{5}\right)$$

    A   -5

    B $-\frac{1}{5}$

    C $\frac{1}{5}$

    D   5

Common Core Standard 7.NS.A.3 – The Number System

☐ **One chocolate bar weighs 0.125 kg. Kevin wants to buy 1 kg of chocolate to make a cake for his mom. How many chocolate bars does Kevin have to buy? Be sure to show your work.**

    A   5

    B   6

    C   7

    D   8

©Teachers' Treasures Publishing

Name_____

PRACTICE

Common Core Standard 7.NS.A.3 – The Number System

☐ Ethan had $26.30 in his wallet. He paid for 2 bottles of water and a chocolate bar. The price of the bottled water was $3.45, and the price of the chocolate bar was $4.75. How much money is left in Ethan's wallet? Be sure to show your work.

A $13.35

B $13.65

C $14.35

D $14.65

Common Core Standard 7.NS.A.3 – The Number System

☐ What is the value of the expression below? Be sure to show your work.

$$\left(2 - \frac{2}{3}\right) \times \left(1 - \frac{1}{4}\right)$$

A $\frac{1}{4}$

B $\frac{1}{3}$

C $\frac{1}{2}$

D   1

Common Core Standard 7.NS.A.3 – The Number System

☐ Benjamin ate $\frac{3}{4}$ kg of grapes. Grace ate $\frac{2}{3}$ as much as Benjamin. How much grapes did Grace eat? Be sure to show your work.

A $\frac{1}{3}$ kg

B $\frac{1}{2}$ kg

C $\frac{3}{5}$ kg

D $\frac{2}{3}$ kg

©Teachers' Treasures Publishing

Name_____

PRACTICE

Common Core Standard 7.NS.A.3 – The Number System

☐ Madison was in the market. She had 2 bags of 0.8 lbs each, and 3 bags of 1.4 lbs each. What is the weight of all bags Madison will carry from the market? Be sure to show your work.

    A   4.2 lbs

    B   4.8 lbs

    C   5.2 lbs

    D   5.8 lbs

Common Core Standard 7.NS.A.3 – The Number System

☐ What is the value of the expression below? Be sure to show your work.

$$\left(2\frac{1}{4} - 1\frac{1}{2}\right) \div \left(1 - \frac{1}{4}\right)$$

    A $\frac{1}{4}$

    B $\frac{1}{2}$

    C   1

    D   2

Common Core Standard 7.NS.A.3 – The Number System

☐ Nadia cut the cake which weighs 4 lb in equal pieces so that each piece weighs $\frac{1}{8}$ lb. How many pieces did Nadia cut? Be sure to show your work.

    A   2

    B   4

    C   12

    D   32

©Teachers' Treasures Publishing

Name_____

ASSESSMENT

Common Core Standard 7.NS.A.3 – The Number System

☐ **Solidat sold 8 bouquets of roses for $51.20. Each bouquet contained 8 roses. How much did one rose cost? Be sure to show your work.**

    A $0.80

    B $1.00

    C $1.20

    D $1.40

Common Core Standard 7.NS.A.3 – The Number System

☐ **What is the value of the expression below? Be sure to show your work.**

$$\left(1\frac{1}{5} + 1\frac{1}{2}\right) \div \frac{9}{10}$$

    A 3

    B $3\frac{1}{10}$

    C $3\frac{1}{5}$

    D $3\frac{1}{2}$

Common Core Standard 7.NS.A.3 – The Number System

☐ **Niseem is 6 ft tall and Priya is $\frac{5}{6}$ as tall as Niseem. How tall is Priya? Be sure to show your work.**

    A   5 ft

    B $5\frac{1}{6}$ ft

    C $5\frac{1}{3}$ ft

    D $5\frac{1}{2}$ ft

©Teachers' Treasures Publishing

Name_____

ASSESSMENT

Common Core Standard 7.NS.A.3 – The Number System

☐ **Rahil has 12 dimes and 16 quarters. How much money does Rahil have altogether? Be sure to show your work.**

    A $4.20

    B $4.60

    C $5.20

    D $5.60

Common Core Standard 7.NS.A.3 – The Number System

☐ **What is the value of the expression below? Be sure to show your work.**

$$3\tfrac{1}{3} - 2\tfrac{1}{2} + 1\tfrac{1}{4}$$

    A $2\tfrac{1}{12}$

    B $2\tfrac{1}{9}$

    C $2\tfrac{1}{8}$

    D $2\tfrac{1}{6}$

Common Core Standard 7.NS.A.3 – The Number System

☐ **A sheep is 3 ft tall and a dog is $\tfrac{2}{3}$ as tall as the sheep. How tall is the dog? Be sure to show your work.**

    A   2 ft

    B $2\tfrac{1}{4}$ ft

    C $2\tfrac{1}{3}$ ft

    D $2\tfrac{1}{2}$ ft

©Teachers' Treasures Publishing

Name_____

DIAGNOSTIC

Common Core Standard 7.EE.A.1 – Expressions & Equations

☐ There are *3c* cars on the parking lot, and each of them has *4* wheels. The expression *4(3c)* represents the total number of wheels on the parking lot. Which of the following expressions also represents the total number of wheels on the parking lot? Be sure to show your work.

A   10c

B   7c

C   12c

D   14c

Common Core Standard 7.EE.A.1 – Expressions & Equations

☐ Which expression is equivalent to the expression below? Be sure to show your work.

$$\frac{3}{4}\left(x - \frac{2}{3}\right)$$

A $\frac{3}{4}x - \frac{1}{2}$

B $\frac{3}{4}x + \frac{1}{2}$

C $-\frac{1}{2}x$

D $\frac{1}{2}x$

Common Core Standard 7.EE.A.1 – Expressions & Equations

☐ Each classroom in the school has *s* students. Sixth graders have 4 classrooms and eighth graders have 3 classrooms. The total number of students is represented by the expression *(4s+3s)*. Which of the following expressions also represents the total number of students? Be sure to show your work.

A   s

B   7s

C   12s

D   43s

©Teachers' Treasures Publishing

Name_____

DIAGNOSTIC

Common Core Standard 7.EE.A.1 – Expressions & Equations

☐ Marsha bought (6p) kg of apples and put them in 2 bags of equal weight. The expression $\left(\frac{6p}{2}\right)$ kg represents the weight of one bag. Which of the following expressions also represents the weight of one bag? Be sure to show your work.

A   p

B   3p

C   4p

D   8p

Common Core Standard 7.EE.A.1 – Expressions & Equations

☐ Which expression is equivalent to the expression below? Be sure to show your work.

$$0.4(8k)$$

A   0.32k

B   3.2k

C   7.6k

D   8.4k

Common Core Standard 7.EE.A.1 – Expressions & Equations

☐ Ryan had *t* toys in the store. He sold $\frac{3}{4}$ of *t* toys. The expression $\left(t - \frac{3}{4}t\right)$ represents the number of toys left in the store. Which of the following expressions also represents the number of toys left in the store? Be sure to show your work.

A $\frac{t}{2}$ C $\frac{t}{4}$

B $\frac{t}{3}$ D $\frac{t}{12}$

©Teachers' Treasures Publishing

Name_____

PRACTICE

Common Core Standard 7.EE.A.1 – Expressions & Equations

☐ **A bottle of soda contains *b* liters of liquid. The expression 8(6b) shows the amount of liquid in 8 six-packs. Which expression also represents the amount of liquid in 8 six-packs? Be sure to show your work.**

- A 2b
- B 14b
- C 48b
- D 86b

Common Core Standard 7.EE.A.1 – Expressions & Equations

☐ **Which expression is equivalent to the expression below? Be sure to show your work.**

$$\frac{10n}{5}$$

- A $\frac{n}{2}$
- B 2n
- C 5n
- D 15n

Common Core Standard 7.EE.A.1 – Expressions & Equations

☐ **Jordan weighs (9w) kg, and Sanjai weighs (3w) kg. The expression (9w+3w) kg shows how much do they weigh together. Which expression also shows how much do Jordan and Sanjai weigh together? Be sure to show your work.**

- A 3w
- B 6w
- C 12w
- D 27w

©Teachers' Treasures Publishing

Name_____

PRACTICE

Common Core Standard 7.EE.A.1 – Expressions & Equations

☐ Four friends shared equally (0.6t) lb of ice cream. The expression $\left(\frac{0.6t}{4}\right)$ lb shows how much ice cream each of the friends received. Which expression also represents that figure? Be sure to show your work.

    A   0.15t

    B   0.24t

    C   0.46t

    D   0.64t

Common Core Standard 7.EE.A.1 – Expressions & Equations

☐ Which expression is equivalent to the expression below? Be sure to show your work.

$$0.7m - 0.2m + 0.6m$$

    A   -m

    B   0.11m

    C   m

    D   1.1m

Common Core Standard 7.EE.A.1 – Expressions & Equations

☐ Katelyn found a stick that was $\left(1\frac{1}{4}n\right)$ yards long. She cut a piece of the stick, so that now it measured $\left(\frac{1}{2}n\right)$ yards long. The expression $\left(1\frac{1}{4}n - \frac{1}{2}n\right)$ yards shows the difference in lengths of the stick before and after Katelyn cut it. Which expression also shows the difference in lengths of the stick? Be sure to show your work.

    A $\frac{1}{8}n$ C $\frac{1}{2}n$

    B $\frac{1}{4}n$ D $\frac{3}{4}n$

Name_____

PRACTICE

Common Core Standard 7.EE.A.1 – Expressions & Equations

☐ There are 8d hens on the farm. The expression 2(8d) represents the total number of legs of hens. Which of the following expressions also represents the total number of legs? Be sure to show your work.

A   4d

B   6d

C   10d

D   16d

Common Core Standard 7.EE.A.1 – Expressions & Equations

☐ Which answer is equivalent to the expression below?

$$0.4(x + 0.5)$$

A $0.4x + 0.9$

B $0.4x + 0.02$

C $0.4x + 0.2$

D $0.4x + 0.09$

Common Core Standard 7.EE.A.1 – Expressions & Equations

☐ Michael and Jordan have *s* boxes each. Michael's boxes weigh 0.75 kg each, and Jordan's boxes weigh 0.5 kg each. The expression (0.75s+0.5s) kg represents the total weight of all boxes. Which of the following expressions also represents the total weight of all boxes? Be sure to show your work.

A   0.25s

B   0.7s

C   0.8s

D   1.25s

Name_____

PRACTICE

Common Core Standard 7.EE.A.1 – Expressions & Equations

☐ There are 12g guests in the hotel. The hotel has only 4-bed rooms, and they are all full with guests. The expression $\frac{12g}{4}$ represents the number of rooms in the hotel. Which expression also represents the number of rooms in the hotel? Be sure to show your work.

A   3g

B   8g

C   16g

D   48g

Common Core Standard 7.EE.A.1 – Expressions & Equations

☐ Which answer is equivalent to the expression below? Be sure to show your work.

$$\frac{2}{3}\left(\frac{3}{5}k\right)$$

A $\frac{2}{15}k$ C $\frac{2}{5}k$

B $\frac{1}{5}k$ D $\frac{1}{3}k$

Common Core Standard 7.EE.A.1 – Expressions & Equations

☐ Calvin had p quarters of dollar. He spent p dimes. The expression 0.25p - 0.1p shows the amount of money left to Calvin. Which expression also shows that amount? Be sure to show your work.

A   0.15p

B   0.24p

C   0.26p

D   0.35p

©Teachers' Treasures Publishing

Name_____

ASSESSMENT

Common Core Standard 7.EE.A.1 – Expressions & Equations

☐ Emma earns $k per hour. She works 8 hours every day. The expression 22(8k) shows her monthly salary. Which expression also shows her monthly salary? Be sure to show your work.

A   14k

B   30k

C   176k

D   228k

Common Core Standard 7.EE.A.1 – Expressions & Equations

☐ Which answer is equivalent to the expression below? Be sure to show your work.

$$\frac{0.75v}{25}$$

A   0.5v

B   0.03v

C   0.3v

D   3v

Common Core Standard 7.EE.A.1 – Expressions & Equations

☐ There are k cars on the parking lot with 4 seats and k cars with 5 seats. The expression (4k+5k) shows the total number of seats. Which expression also shows the total number of seats? Be sure to show your work.

A   k

B   9k

C   20k

D   45k

©Teachers' Treasures Publishing

Name_____

ASSESSMENT

Common Core Standard 7.EE.A.1 – Expressions & Equations

☐ The fabric the length of which is (0.8r) yards is cut in 4 equal pieces. The expression $\left(\frac{0.8}{4}r\right)$ yards shows the length of each of the 5 pieces. Which expression also shows the length of each piece? Be sure to show your work.

A   0.2r

B   0.4r

C   0.48r

D   0.84r

Common Core Standard 7.EE.A.1 – Expressions & Equations

☐ Which answer is equivalent to the expression below? Be sure to show your work.

$$\frac{1}{2}t + \frac{1}{3}t - \frac{1}{4}t$$

A $\frac{1}{9}t$ C $\frac{1}{3}t$

B $\frac{1}{12}t$ D $\frac{7}{12}t$

Common Core Standard 7.EE.A.1 – Expressions & Equations

☐ The school is (2.3k) miles away from the library, and (1.9k) miles away from the post office. The expression (2.3k-1.9k) shows how many miles the library is closer to the school than it is to the post office. Which expression also shows how many miles the library is closer to the school than to the post office? Be sure to show your work.

A   0.4k

B   1.4k

C   3.2k

D   4.2k

©Teachers' Treasures Publishing

Name_____

DIAGNOSTIC

Common Core Standard 7.EE.A.2 – Expressions & Equations

☐ Cameron is selling shirts. The price of each shirt was *k* dollars, but Cameron decided to increase the price by 7%. The expression (k+0.07k) represents the new price of the shirts. Which expression also represents that price? Be sure to show your work.

 A   k+7%

 B   1.07k

 C $0.07k^2$

 D   7%k

Common Core Standard 7.EE.A.2 – Expressions & Equations

☐ Which expression is equivalent to the sentence below? Be sure to show your work.

"p is decreased by 9%"

 A   0.09p

 B   1.09p

 C   0.1p

 D   0.91p

Common Core Standard 7.EE.A.2 – Expressions & Equations

☐ The dimensions of the football field are *p* and *q*. The expression 2p+2q represents the perimeter of the the football field. Which expression also represents the perimeter of the the football field? Be sure to show your work.

 A   2(p+q)

 B   2pq

 C   4pq

 D   4(p+q)

Name_____

DIAGNOSTIC

Common Core Standard 7.EE.A.2 – Expressions & Equations

☐ The profit of Larry's company was p dollars last year. The profit decreased by 6% this year. The expression (p-6%p) represents the profit made this year. Which expression also represents the profit made this year? Be sure to show your work.

- A   0.4p
- B   0.6p
- C   0.94p
- D   1.06p

Common Core Standard 7.EE.A.2 – Expressions & Equations

☐ Which expression is equivalent to the sentence below? Be sure to show your work.

"k is increased by 4%"

- A   k+0.04k
- B   k+0.4k
- C   k+4k
- D   k+400k

Common Core Standard 7.EE.A.2 – Expressions & Equations

☐ There are h hens and s sheep on the farm. The expression (2h+4s) represents the total number of their legs. Which expression also represents the total number of their legs? Be sure to show your work.

- A   2(h+s)
- B   4(h+s)
- C   6hs
- D   2(h+2s)

Name_____

PRACTICE

Common Core Standard 7.EE.A.2 – Expressions & Equations

☐ **Darchelle works as a babysitter. She earns s dollars monthly. Next month her monthly salary will be increased by 12%. The expression 1.12s represents her future salary. Which expression also represents her future salary? Be sure to show your work.**

A   s+12s

B   s+0.12s

C   s+0.12

D   s+12%

Common Core Standard 7.EE.A.2 – Expressions & Equations

☐ **Which expression is equivalent to the sentence below? Be sure to show your work.**

"k is decreased by 26%"

A   -0.26k

B   0.74k

C   74k

D   -26k

Common Core Standard 7.EE.A.2 – Expressions & Equations

☐ **There are t six-packs of soda and v four-packs of juice. The expression (6t+4v) represents the total number of bottled drinks. Which expression also represents the total number of bottled drinks? Be sure to show your work.**

A   4(2t+v)

B   24tv

C   10tv

D   2(3t+2v)

Name_____

PRACTICE

Common Core Standard 7.EE.A.2 – Expressions & Equations

☐ Cindy's dog weighed *t* lb before she started a new diet. Then she lost 15% of her weight. The expression (t-15%t) represents Cindy's dog's new weight. Which expression also represents her new weight? Be sure to show your work.

A   -0.15t

B   0.85t

C   -15%t

D   85t

Common Core Standard 7.EE.A.2 – Expressions & Equations

☐ Which expression is equivalent to the sentence below? Be sure to show your work.

"n is increased by 34%"

A   n+0.34n

B   34n

C   0.34n

D   n+34n

Common Core Standard 7.EE.A.2 – Expressions & Equations

☐ There are *t* triangles and *h* hexagons in the outline of a plane. The expression (3t+6h) represents the total number of their sides. Which expression also represents the total number of their sides? Be sure to show your work.

A   3(t+2h)

B   9th

C   18th

D   3(t+h)

Name _____

PRACTICE

Common Core Standard 7.EE.A.2 – Expressions & Equations

☐ Christine is reselling books. She buys books for *n* dollars and then marks them up by 5% each. The expression (n+0.05n) represents the new price of each book. Which expression also represents this price? Be sure to show your work.

A   0.6n

B   0.06n

C   1.5n

D   1.05n

Common Core Standard 7.EE.A.2 – Expressions & Equations

☐ Which expression is equivalent to the sentence below? Be sure to show your work.

"p is decreased by 6.5%"

A   0.935p

B   93.5p

C   0.35p

D   35p

Common Core Standard 7.EE.A.2 – Expressions & Equations

☐ The dimensions of Martha's new furniture piece are *w* and *h*. The expression 2(w+h) represents the perimeter of the furniture. Which expression also represents this perimeter? Be sure to show your work.

A   2w+h

B   w+2h

C   2wh

D   2w+2h

©Teachers' Treasures Publishing

Name_____

PRACTICE

Common Core Standard 7.EE.A.2 – Expressions & Equations

☐ Nikita's savings in the bank was equivalent to *p* dollars last year. The savings decreased by 4% this year. The expression 0.96p represents Nikita's savings this year. Which expression also represents the savings this year? Be sure to show your work.

A   p−0.4p

B   p−0.04p

C   p−4%

D   p−4p

Common Core Standard 7.EE.A.2 – Expressions & Equations

☐ Which expression is equivalent to the sentence below? Be sure to show your work.

"k is increased by 120%"

A   k+0.12k

B   k+1.2k

C   k+12k

D   k+120k

Common Core Standard 7.EE.A.2 – Expressions & Equations

☐ There are *b* bikes and *c* cars on Main Street. The expression (2b+4c) represents the total number of their wheels. Which expression also represents the total number of the wheels on Main Street? Be sure to show your work.

A   2(b+2c)

B   4(b+c)

C   2(b+c)

D   6bc

©Teachers' Treasures Publishing

Name_____

ASSESSMENT

Common Core Standard 7.EE.A.2 – Expressions & Equations

☐ **Petros drives a car at a speed of *s* miles per hour. He increased the speed by 30% in the last 10 minutes. The expression 1.3s represents his increased speed. Which expression also represents the current speed? Be sure to show your work.**

  A s+30s

  B s+3s

  C s+0.3s

  D s+30%

Common Core Standard 7.EE.A.2 – Expressions & Equations

☐ **Which expression is equivalent to the sentence below? Be sure to show your work.**

"k is decreased by 0.8%"

  A 0.92k

  B 0.2k

  C 92k

  D 0.992k

Common Core Standard 7.EE.A.2 – Expressions & Equations

☐ **Alejandra bought *t* bottles of 1 liter apple juice and *v* bottles of 2 liter orange juice. The expression (t+2v) represents the total number of liters of juice. Which expression also represents that number? Be sure to show your work.**

  A 2(2t+v)

  B 2(t+v)

  C 2(0.5t+v)

  D 2(2t+2v)

©Teachers' Treasures Publishing

Name_____

ASSESSMENT

Common Core Standard 7.EE.A.2 – Expressions & Equations

☐ Jackson's pants were *k* feet long. He cut 25% from the bottom of his pants, and now they fit perfectly. The expression (k-25%k) represents the new length of Jackson's pants. Which expression also represents the new length of pants? Be sure to show your work.

A   0.75k

B   -24%k

C   -25k

D   0.25k

Common Core Standard 7.EE.A.2 – Expressions & Equations

☐ Which expression is equivalent to the sentence below? Be sure to show your work.

"n is increased by 200%"

A   2n

B   3n

C   200n

D   300n

Common Core Standard 7.EE.A.2 – Expressions & Equations

☐ The expression (4t+8c) represents the total number of vertices of *t* tetrahedrons and *c* cubes. Which expression also represents the total number of their vertices? Be sure to show your work.

A   12tc

B   32tc

C   4(t+2c)

D   4(t+4c)

©Teachers' Treasures Publishing

Name_____

DIAGNOSTIC

Common Core Standard 7.EE.B.3 – Expressions & Equations

☐ A six-pack of soda costs $12.90. What is the price of one bottle of soda? Be sure to show your work.

A $2.15

B $2.20

C $2.25

D $2.30

Common Core Standard 7.EE.B.3 – Expressions & Equations

☐ Write 0.16 as a fraction in lowest terms. Be sure to show your work.

A $\frac{1}{6}$

B $\frac{1}{16}$

C $\frac{4}{25}$

D $\frac{8}{5}$

Common Core Standard 7.EE.B.3 – Expressions & Equations

☐ A car factory builds 83 cars each day. How many cars will the factory build in 28 days? Choose the best estimate. Be sure to show your work.

A 5,000

B 3,000

C 2,400

D 1,600

©Teachers' Treasures Publishing

Name_____

DIAGNOSTIC

Common Core Standard 7.EE.B.3 – Expressions & Equations

☐ Elizabeth had $240 before she started shopping. She spent 20% of her money within the first hour. How much money will Elizabeth have after the first hour of shopping? Be sure to show your work.

A $48

B $192

C $216

D $220

Common Core Standard 7.EE.B.3 – Expressions & Equations

☐ Write $\frac{3}{4}$ as a decimal number. Be sure to show your work.

A   0.34

B   0.43

C   0.75

D   3.4

Common Core Standard 7.EE.B.3 – Expressions & Equations

☐ The bag of apples weighs 3.3 kg, and a bag of apricots weighs $3\frac{1}{4}$ kg. How much heavier is the bag of apples compared to the bag of apricots? Be sure to show your work.

A $\frac{1}{3}$ kg

B $\frac{1}{4}$ kg

C $\frac{1}{10}$ kg

D $\frac{1}{20}$ kg

©Teachers' Treasures Publishing

Name_____

PRACTICE

Common Core Standard 7.EE.B.3 – Expressions & Equations

☐ Timothy has 7 boxes of shoes and 4 boxes of shirts. Each box of shoes contains 5 pairs of shoes, and each box of shirts contains 9 shirts. How many more shirts shoes does Timothy have? Be sure to show your work.

A 1

B 2

C 3

D 4

Common Core Standard 7.EE.B.3 – Expressions & Equations

☐ What is the value of the expression below? Be sure to show your work.

$$3\frac{4}{5} - 1\frac{3}{4}$$

A 1

B $1\frac{1}{20}$

C 2

D $2\frac{1}{20}$

Common Core Standard 7.EE.B.3 – Expressions & Equations

☐ Look at the map below. What is the distance from A to C via B? Be sure to show your work.

A 9.1 mi

B 9.5 mi

C 10.1 mi

D 10.5 mi

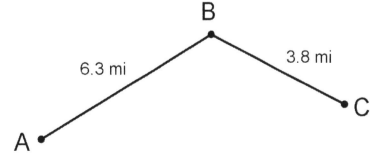

©Teachers' Treasures Publishing

Name _____

PRACTICE

Common Core Standard 7.EE.B.3 – Expressions & Equations

☐ Silva read $\frac{4}{5}$ of the book that has a total of 165 pages. How many pages did she read? Be sure to show your work.

- A   130
- B   131
- C   132
- D   133

Common Core Standard 7.EE.B.3 – Expressions & Equations

☐ Simplify the expression below and mark the correct answer. Be sure to show your work.

$$1 - 0.23 + 0.48$$

- A   0.25
- B   0.29
- C   1.25
- D   1.29

Common Core Standard 7.EE.B.3 – Expressions & Equations

☐ Jacob has $1.90. He has 10 coins, all dimes and quarters. How many dimes and quarters does he have? Be sure to show your work.

- A   6 quarters, 4 dimes
- B   4 quarters, 6 dimes
- C   7 quarters, 3 dimes
- D   3 quarters, 7 dimes

©Teachers' Treasures Publishing

Name _____

PRACTICE

Common Core Standard 7.EE.B.3 – Expressions & Equations

☐ A bag of licorice costs $2.35 and a pack of chewing gum costs $0.80. Valerie bought 2 bags of licorice and 3 packs of chewing gum. How much did she pay? Be sure to show your work.

    A $7.10

    B $7.65

    C $8.10

    D $8.65

Common Core Standard 7.EE.B.3 – Expressions & Equations

☐ Write 0.222… as a fraction in lowest terms and mark the correct answer. Be sure to show your work.

    A $\frac{1}{5}$

    B $\frac{2}{9}$

    C $\frac{11}{50}$

    D $\frac{1}{9}$

Common Core Standard 7.EE.B.3 – Expressions & Equations

☐ The 7th grade math teacher creates 32 test questions each day. How many test questions does she create in 28 days? Choose the best estimate. Be sure to show your work.

    A   500

    B   1,000

    C   2,000

    D   4,000

©Teachers' Treasures Publishing

Name_____

PRACTICE

Common Core Standard 7.EE.B.3 – Expressions & Equations

☐ Gretta earns $20 per hour working as a babysitter. Starting from the next month, she will be paid 40% more. How much will Gretta earn per hour? Be sure to show your work.

- A $24
- B $28
- C $40
- D $60

Common Core Standard 7.EE.B.3 – Expressions & Equations

☐ Write 56% as a decimal number and mark the correct answer. Be sure to show your work.

- A 0.5
- B 0.56
- C 0.6
- D 5.6

Common Core Standard 7.EE.B.3 – Expressions & Equations

☐ A cicada is 1.4 in long, while a grasshopper is $1\frac{1}{2}$ in long. How much longer is the grasshopper than the cicada? Be sure to show your work.

- A $\frac{1}{2}$ in
- B $\frac{1}{4}$ in
- C $\frac{1}{10}$ in
- D $\frac{1}{20}$ in

Name_____

ASSESSMENT

Common Core Standard 7.EE.B.3 – Expressions & Equations

☐ There are 8 basketball teams and 7 volleyball teams at the sports camp. Each basketball team has 5 players, and each volleyball team has 6 players. How many more volleyball players than basketball players are at the sports camp? Be sure to show your work.

A   1

B   2

C   13

D   26

Common Core Standard 7.EE.B.3 – Expressions & Equations

☐ What is the value of the expression below? Be sure to show your work.

$$1\frac{2}{3} + 2\frac{1}{4}$$

A $3\frac{11}{12}$

B $3\frac{3}{7}$

C $4\frac{11}{12}$

D $4\frac{3}{7}$

Common Core Standard 7.EE.B.3 – Expressions & Equations

☐ Look at the map below. The distance from A to C via B is 10.4 miles. What is the distance from A to B? Be sure to show your work.

A   5.3 mi

B   5.7 mi

C   6.3 mi

D   6.7 mi

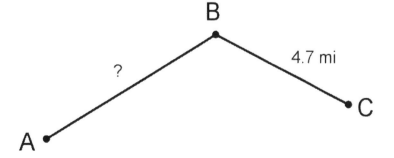

©Teachers' Treasures Publishing

Name_____

ASSESSMENT

Common Core Standard 7.EE.B.3 – Expressions & Equations

☐ The distance between two cities is 120 miles. Janette is driving a car. She passed $\frac{2}{3}$ of the distance between the cities. How many miles did Janette pass? Be sure to show your work.

A   40 mi

B   60 mi

C   80 mi

D   100 mi

Common Core Standard 7.EE.B.3 – Expressions & Equations

☐ Simplify expression below and mark the correct answer. Be sure to show your work.

$$0.35 - 0.8 + 0.3$$

A   -0.75

B   -0.15

C   0.15

D   0.75

Common Core Standard 7.EE.B.3 – Expressions & Equations

☐ Skylar has 2.6 kg of buiscuits in 10 different packs, of which some are 0.25 kg and some 0.3 kg. How many packs of 0.25 kg and 0.3 kg does Skylar have? Be sure to show your work.

A   2 packs of 0.25 kg, 8 packs of 0.3 kg

B   4 packs of 0.25 kg, 6 packs of 0.3 kg

C   6 packs of 0.25 kg, 4 packs of 0.3 kg

D   8 packs of 0.25 kg, 2 packs of 0.3 kg

Name_____

DIAGNOSTIC

Common Core Standard 7.EE.B.4.A – Expressions & Equations

☐ There are 57 cars on the parking lot. They are arranged in 7 rows: *x* cars are in each of 6 rows, and 3 cars are in the last row. What is the value of *x*? Be sure to show your work.

    A   6

    B   7

    C   8

    D   9

Common Core Standard 7.EE.B.4.A – Expressions & Equations

☐ Solve for *x* in the expression below and mark the correct answer. Be sure to show your work.

$$\frac{2}{3}\left(x - \frac{1}{2}\right) = \frac{1}{6}$$

    A $\frac{1}{4}$ C $\frac{2}{3}$

    B $\frac{1}{3}$ D $\frac{3}{4}$

Common Core Standard 7.EE.B.4.A – Expressions & Equations

☐ The perimeter of the swimming pool is 150 m, and its length is 50 m. What is the width of the swimming pool? Be sure to show your work.

    A   10 m

    B   15 m

    C   25 m

    D   30 m

Name_____

DIAGNOSTIC

Common Core Standard 7.EE.B.4.A – Expressions & Equations

☐ **There are 44 flowers in the flower garden. They are arranged in 6 rows: *x* flowers are in each of 5 rows, and 4 flowers are in the last row. What is the value of *x*? Be sure to show your work.**

A 6

B 7

C 8

D 9

Common Core Standard 7.EE.B.4.A – Expressions & Equations

☐ **Solve for *x* in the expression below and mark the correct answer. Be sure to show your work.**

$$0.5x + 3 = 4.2$$

A 2.2

B 2.4

C 2.6

D 2.8

Common Core Standard 7.EE.B.4.A – Expressions & Equations

☐ **12 dogs and *x* cats together have 68 legs. How many cats are there? Be sure to show your work.**

A 5

B 6

C 7

D 8

©Teachers' Treasures Publishing

Name_____

PRACTICE

Common Core Standard 7.EE.B.4.A – Expressions & Equations

☐ Mr. Moody creates math test questions 5 days in a week. He works x hours every day, except Friday, when he works 2.5 hours. If he works 22.5 hours per week, what is the value of x? Be sure to show your work.

    A   5

    B   6

    C   7

    D   8

Common Core Standard 7.EE.B.4.A – Expressions & Equations

☐ Solve for x in the expression below and mark the correct answer. Be sure to show your work.

$$0.2(x + 5) = 1.4$$

    A   1

    B   2

    C   3

    D   4

Common Core Standard 7.EE.B.4.A – Expressions & Equations

☐ 9 bicycles and x bikes together have 32 wheels. How many bikes are there? Be sure to show your work.

    A   7

    B   8

    C   9

    D   10

©Teachers' Treasures Publishing

Name_____

PRACTICE

Common Core Standard 7.EE.B.4.A – Expressions & Equations

☐ The weight of 9 boxes is 100 kg. Each box weighs x kg, except one that weighs 4 kg. What is the value of x? Be sure to show your work.

A   10 kg

B   11 kg

C   12 kg

D   13 kg

Common Core Standard 7.EE.B.4.A – Expressions & Equations

☐ Solve for x in the expression below and mark the correct answer. Be sure to show your work.

$$\frac{1}{2}x - \frac{1}{3} = 1$$

A $1\frac{1}{3}$

B $1\frac{2}{3}$

C $2\frac{1}{3}$

D $2\frac{2}{3}$

Common Core Standard 7.EE.B.4.A – Expressions & Equations

☐ How wide is the tennis court the length of which is 78 ft, and perimeter is 228 ft? Be sure to show your work.

A   26 ft

B   36 ft

C   46 ft

D   56 ft

Name _____

PRACTICE

Common Core Standard 7.EE.B.4.A – Expressions & Equations

☐ 37 soldiers are arranged in 6 rows. There are x soldiers in each row, except the last row, where there are 2 soldiers. What is the value of x? Be sure to show your work.

A   6

B   7

C   8

D   9

Common Core Standard 7.EE.B.4.A – Expressions & Equations

☐ Solve for x in the expression below and mark the correct answer. Be sure to show your work.

$$\frac{1}{2}(x + 0.2) = 1$$

A   1.2

B   1.4

C   1.6

D   1.8

Common Core Standard 7.EE.B.4.A – Expressions & Equations

☐ The perimeter of the basketball court is 87.78 m, and its width is 15.24 m. What is the length of the basketball court? Be sure to show your work.

A   28.35 m

B   28.65 m

C   29.35 m

D   29.65 m

©Teachers' Treasures Publishing

Name_____

PRACTICE

Common Core Standard 7.EE.B.4.A – Expressions & Equations

☐ There are 50 apple trees in the orchard. They are arranged in 8 rows: *x* trees are in each of 7 rows, and only 1 tree is in the last row. What is the value of *x*?   Be sure to show your work.

A   6

B   7

C   8

D   9

Common Core Standard 7.EE.B.4.A – Expressions & Equations

☐ Solve for *x* in the expresson below and mark the correct answer. Be sure to show your work.

$$0.25x - \frac{1}{2} = 1$$

A   3

B   4

C   5

D   6

Common Core Standard 7.EE.B.4.A – Expressions & Equations

☐ Cole pays $20 per hour each for his two workers. This week they worked 40 hours and *x* hours each. Cole paid them $1,200. What is the value of *x*? Be sure to show your work.

A   20

B   25

C   30

D   35

Name_____

ASSESSMENT

Common Core Standard 7.EE.B.4.A – Expressions & Equations

☐ Angela read 127 pages of a book in 5 days. First 4 days she read *x* pages every day, and last day she read 15 pages. What is the value of *x*? Be sure to show your work.

    A   25

    B   26

    C   27

    D   28

Common Core Standard 7.EE.B.4.A – Expressions & Equations

☐ Solve for *x* in the expression below and mark the correct answer. Be sure to show your work.

$$0.2\left(x + \frac{1}{3}\right) = 2$$

    A $8\frac{1}{3}$ C $9\frac{1}{3}$

    B $8\frac{2}{3}$ D $9\frac{2}{3}$

Common Core Standard 7.EE.B.4.A – Expressions & Equations

☐ 8 ducks and *x* hens on the farm together have 54 legs. How many hens are on the farm? Be sure to show your work.

    A   17

    B   18

    C   19

    D   20

©Teachers' Treasures Publishing

Name_____

ASSESSMENT

Common Core Standard 7.EE.B.4.A – Expressions & Equations

☐ **Jim has 38 bottles of water in 9 packs of *x* bottles and one pack that contains only 2 bottles. What is the value of *x*? Be sure to show your work.**

    A   3

    B   4

    C   5

    D   6

Common Core Standard 7.EE.B.4.A – Expressions & Equations

☐ **Solve for *x* in the expression below and mark the correct answer. Be sure to show your work.**

$$2x - \frac{1}{2} = 2$$

    A $1\frac{1}{4}$

    B $1\frac{1}{2}$

    C $1\frac{3}{4}$

    D   2

Common Core Standard 7.EE.B.4.A – Expressions & Equations

☐ **How wide is the room the length of which is 5 yards, and perimeter is 16 yards? Be sure to show your work.**

    A   3 yards

    B   5 yards

    C   8 yards

    D   11 yards

©Teachers' Treasures Publishing

Name_____

DIAGNOSTIC

Common Core Standard 7.EE.B.4.B – Expressions & Equations

☐ **Jackie has 5 bottles of lemonade on her lemonade stand. In order to raise money for her dance club, she needs at least 100. A pack of lemonade contains 12 bottles. How many packs of lemonade does Jackie need to get to her minimum number? Be sure to show your work.**

- A 6
- B 7
- C 8
- D 9

Common Core Standard 7.EE.B.4.B – Expressions & Equations

☐ **Solve for *x* in the expression below and mark the correct answer. Be sure to show your work.**

$$\frac{1}{2}x - 1 < 3$$

- A x < 2
- B x > 2
- C x < 8
- D x > 8

Common Core Standard 7.EE.B.4.B – Expressions & Equations

☐ **There are 3 bikes and *x* cars in the body shop. What must be the greatest number of cars, so that the total number of wheels is less than 31? Be sure to show your work.**

- A 5
- B 6
- C 7
- D 8

Name_____

DIAGNOSTIC

Common Core Standard 7.EE.B.4.B – Expressions & Equations

☐   **Shevan has 100 flowers. How many bouquets of 7 flowers can she make? Be sure to show your work.**

    A   14

    B   15

    C   16

    D   17

Common Core Standard 7.EE.B.4.B – Expressions & Equations

☐   **Solve for *x* in the expression below and mark the correct answer. Be sure to show your work.**

$$0.3x - 0.2 > 1$$

    A $x > 3$

    B $x > 4$

    C $x > 5$

    D $x > 6$

Common Core Standard 7.EE.B.4.B – Expressions & Equations

☐   **Tigran wants to pay a bill of $28 with banknotes of $5. What is the least number of banknotes he will need? Be sure to show your work.**

    A   5

    B   6

    C   7

    D   8

©Teachers' Treasures Publishing

Name_____

PRACTICE

Common Core Standard 7.EE.B.4.B – Expressions & Equations

☐ The cab driver charges $5 start fee and $3 for every travel mile. Write an inequality for the greatest number of miles that cab driver will drive for $30. Be sure to show your work.

A $3x + 5 \leq 30$

B $3x + 5 \geq 30$

C $5x + 3 \leq 30$

D $5x + 3 \geq 30$

Common Core Standard 7.EE.B.4.B – Expressions & Equations

☐ Solve for *x* in the expression below and mark the correct answer. Be sure to show your work.

$$\frac{1}{3}x + \frac{1}{2} > \frac{1}{6}$$

A $x > -1$

B $x < -1$

C $x > 1$

D $x < 1$

Common Core Standard 7.EE.B.4.B – Expressions & Equations

☐ Addison read 25 pages of the book first day. She continued to read 20 pages every day. The book has 245 pages. Write an inequality for the least number of days Addison will need to finish the book. Be sure to show your work.

A $25x + 20 \geq 245$

B $25x + 20 \leq 245$

C $20x + 25 \geq 245$

D $20x + 25 \leq 245$

Name_____

PRACTICE

Common Core Standard 7.EE.B.4.B – Expressions & Equations

☐ **Bart wants to buy at least 50 fruit snacks for the Valentine's treats. One fruit snack pack contains 6 pieces. Write an inequality for the least number of fruit snack Bart will need to buy. Be sure to show your work.**

A $50x \leq 6$

B $50x \geq 6$

C $6x \leq 50$

D $6x \geq 50$

Common Core Standard 7.EE.B.4.B – Expressions & Equations

☐ **Solve for *x* in the expression below and mark the correct answer. Be sure to show your work.**

$$1.4x + 0.1 < 2.9$$

A $x > 1$

B $x < 1$

C $x > 2$

D $x < 2$

Common Core Standard 7.EE.B.4.B – Expressions & Equations

☐ **Mainland traveling basketball teams have 5 players. There are 37 beds in the En-Route motel. Write an inequality for the greatest number of basketball teams that can be settled in the motel. Be sure to show your work.**

A $37x \leq 5$

B $37x \geq 5$

C $5x \leq 37$

D $5x \geq 37$

Name_____

PRACTICE

Common Core Standard 7.EE.B.4.B – Expressions & Equations

☐ To open a restaurant Heather needs at least 80 plates. She has only 7 plates at the moment. A set of plates contains 6 plates. At least how many sets of plates does Heather need to open her restaurant? Be sure to show your work.

    A   11

    B   12

    C   13

    D   14

Common Core Standard 7.EE.B.4.B – Expressions & Equations

☐ Solve for *x* in the expression below and mark the correct answer. Be sure to show your work.

$$2 - \frac{1}{2}x < \frac{1}{3}$$

    A $x < 3\frac{1}{3}$

    B $x > 3\frac{1}{3}$

    C $x < 2\frac{1}{3}$

    D $x > 2\frac{1}{3}$

Common Core Standard 7.EE.B.4.B – Expressions & Equations

☐ There are 5 turkeys and *x* goats on the Bobby's farm. What must be the greatest number of goats, so that the total number of all farm animal legs is less than 60? Be sure to show your work.

    A   9

    B   10

    C   11

    D   12

Name_____

PRACTICE

Common Core Standard 7.EE.B.4.B – Expressions & Equations

☐ How many football teams can be created of 50 players, if each football team consists of 11 players? Be sure to show your work.

    A   4

    B   5

    C   6

    D   7

Common Core Standard 7.EE.B.4.B – Expressions & Equations

☐ Solve for x in the expression below and mark the correct answer. Be sure to show your work.

$$0.4 - 0.5x > 3$$

    A $x > 5.2$

    B $x < 5.2$

    C $x > -5.2$

    D $x < -5.2$

Common Core Standard 7.EE.B.4.B – Expressions & Equations

☐ Maya's grocery store bill is $46. She only has banknotes of $10. What is the least number of banknotes she will need to pay for her grocery bill? Be sure to show your work.

    A   4

    B   5

    C   6

    D   10

Name_____

ASSESSMENT

Common Core Standard 7.EE.B.4.B – Expressions & Equations

☐ An international phone company charges $20 monthly flat fee and $0.15 for every minute of call. Write an inequality for the greatest number of minutes one can talk for $35. Be sure to show your work.

- A $0.15x + 20 \leq 35$
- B $0.15x + 20 \geq 35$
- C $20x + 0.15 \leq 35$
- D $20x + 0.15 \geq 35$

Common Core Standard 7.EE.B.4.B – Expressions & Equations

☐ Solve for *x* in the expression below and mark the correct answer. Be sure to show your work.

$$\frac{1}{4} > 1 + \frac{x}{2}$$

- A $x > -1\frac{1}{2}$
- B $x < -1\frac{1}{2}$
- C $x > 1\frac{1}{2}$
- D $x < 1\frac{1}{2}$

Common Core Standard 7.EE.B.4.B – Expressions & Equations

☐ Benjamin drives to his friend's party at a speed of 40 miles per hour. He already passed 50 miles. The total distance he needs to pass is 324 miles. Write an inequality for the least number of hours Benjamin needs to arrive at his friend's party. Be sure to show your work.

- A $50x + 40 \geq 324$
- B $50x + 40 \leq 324$
- C $40x + 50 \geq 324$
- D $40x + 50 \leq 324$

©Teachers' Treasures Publishing

Name_____

ASSESSMENT

Common Core Standard 7.EE.B.4.B – Expressions & Equations

☐ **Chez Lusinè's Bakery sells at least 200 loaves of breads per day. The bakery oven bakes 30 loaves per hour. Write an inequality for the least number of hours needed to bake 200 loaves. Be sure to show your work.**

- A $30x \leq 200$
- B $30x \geq 200$
- C $200x \leq 30$
- D $200x \geq 30$

Common Core Standard 7.EE.B.4.B – Expressions & Equations

☐ **Solve for *x* in the expression below and mark the correct answer. Be sure to show your work.**

$$0.2 < 1.2x + 2.6$$

- A $x > -2$
- B $x < -2$
- C $x > 2$
- D $x < 2$

Common Core Standard 7.EE.B.4.B – Expressions & Equations

☐ **Write an inequality for the greatest number of six-packs that can be created of 86 bottles of water. Be sure to show your work.**

- A $86x \leq 6$
- B $86x \geq 6$
- C $6x \leq 86$
- D $6x \geq 86$

©Teachers' Treasures Publishing

Name_____

DIAGNOSTIC

Common Core Standard 7.G.A.1 – Geometry

☐ Erik made a scaled drawing of the tree in the park. In Erik's drawing the tree is 6 inches tall. If the scale factor is 1:36, how tall is the actual tree in yards? Be sure to show your work.

  A 3 yards

  B 4 yards

  C 5 yards

  D 6 yards

Common Core Standard 7.G.A.1 – Geometry

☐ If AB||DE, what is the measure of α? Be sure to show your work.

  A $35°$

  B $45°$

  C $55°$

  D $135°$

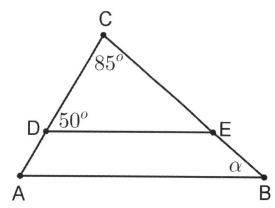

Common Core Standard 7.G.A.1 – Geometry

☐ The width of a window treatment is 26 yards, and its length is 30 yards. If the dimensions of the windows are halved, what would be the ratio of areas of the new and old window treatments? Be sure to show your work.

  A 1:4

  B 4:1

  C 1:2

  D 2:1

Name_____

DIAGNOSTIC

Common Core Standard 7.G.A.1 – Geometry

☐ A scaled picture of a car is 20 cm long. The actual car is 5 m long in real life. What is the scale factor? Be sure to show your work.

A   2:5

B   1:25

C   5:2

D   25:1

Common Core Standard 7.G.A.1 – Geometry

☐ What is the length of AB? Be sure to show your work.

A   7 in

B   8 in

C   9 in

D   10 in

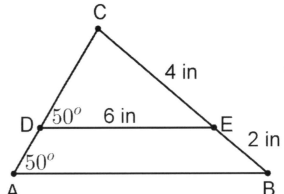

Common Core Standard 7.G.A.1 – Geometry

☐ The drawing below represents a park. What is the area of the park, if the scale factor is 1:100? Be sure to show your work.

A   100 cm²

B   1,000 cm²

C   100 m²

D   1,000 m²

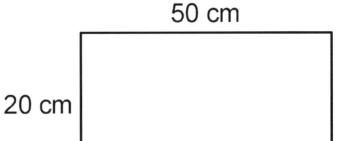

©Teachers' Treasures Publishing   Page 162

Name_____

PRACTICE

Common Core Standard 7.G.A.1 – Geometry

☐ At a museum, Elaine was impressed by a 6-yd high fabric needlework. Elaine decided to make a drawing of this artwork so that 1 inch in the drawing represents 1 foot of the actual artwork. How high will be Elaine's drawing? Be sure to show your work.

A   1 ft

B $1\frac{1}{2}$ ft

C   2 ft

D $2\frac{1}{2}$ ft

Common Core Standard 7.G.A.1 – Geometry

☐ The triangles below are similar. What is the value of *x*? Be sure to show your work.

A   7.5 in

B   8 in

C   10 in

D   12.5 in

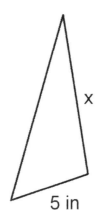

Common Core Standard 7.G.A.1 – Geometry

☐ The drawing below represents a daycare playground. What is the area of the playground in real life? Be sure to show your work.

A   192 m²

B   216 m²

C   288 m²

D   432 m²

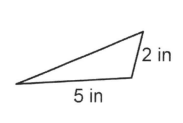

©Teachers' Treasures Publishing

Name_____

PRACTICE

Common Core Standard 7.G.A.1 – Geometry

☐ 1 cm on a large state map represents an actual distance of 5 km. The distance between two cities on the map is 23 cm. What is the actual distance between the two cities? Be sure to show your work.

A   5 km

B   23 km

C   28 km

D   115 km

Common Core Standard 7.G.A.1 – Geometry

☐ The triangles below are similar. What is the measure of α? Be sure to show your work.

A   20°

B   80°

C   100°

D   120°

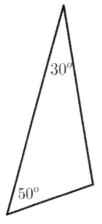

Common Core Standard 7.G.A.1 – Geometry

☐ The drawing below represents a swimming pool. What is the area of the actual swimming pool in real life? Be sure to show your work.

A   200 m²

B   1,250 m²

C   2,000 m²

D   12,500 m²

©Teachers' Treasures Publishing

Common Core Standard 7.G.A.1 – Geometry

☐ Logan made a scaled drawing of his dog. In Logan's drawing the dog is 10 inches tall. If the scale factor is 5:12, how tall is Logan's dog? Be sure to show your work.

A   1 ft

B $1\frac{1}{2}$ ft

C   2 ft

D $2\frac{1}{2}$ ft

Common Core Standard 7.G.A.1 – Geometry

☐ What is the measure of α? Be sure to show your work.

A 35^0

B $40°$

C $45°$

D $50°$

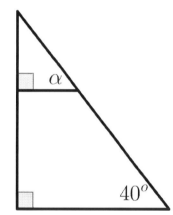

Common Core Standard 7.G.A.1 – Geometry

☐ The height of a picture frame is 2 ft, and its length is 5 ft. If the dimensions of the picture frame are doubled, what is the ratio of areas of the new and the old picture frames? Be sure to show your work.

A   1:4

B   4:1

C   1:2

D   2:1

©Teachers' Treasures Publishing

Name_____

PRACTICE

Common Core Standard 7.G.A.1 – Geometry

☐ A scaled drawing of a boat is 80 cm long. The actual length of the boat is 12 m. What is the scale factor? Be sure to show your work.

A   1:12

B   1:15

C   1:80

D   2:3

Common Core Standard 7.G.A.1 – Geometry

☐ What is the value of x? Be sure to show your work.

A   3 in

B   4 in

C   6 in

D   7 in

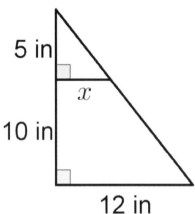

Common Core Standard 7.G.A.1 – Geometry

☐ The drawing below represents a kitchen floor. What is the area of the kitchen floor, if the scale factor is 3:40? Be sure to show your work.

A   8 m^2

B   10 m^2

C   12 m^2

D   14 m^2

45 cm

15 cm

©Teachers' Treasures Publishing

Name _____

ASSESSMENT

Common Core Standard 7.G.A.1 – Geometry

☐ Julia bought 8 yards of fabric. She wants to draw a picture for the seamstress of a new backdrop for her photo studio, so that 1 inch in her drawing represents 2 feet in real life. How big will be Julia's picture? Be sure to show your work.

A   4 in

B   6 in

C   8 in

D   12 in

Common Core Standard 7.G.A.1 – Geometry

☐ The triangles below are similar. What is the value of x? Be sure to show your work.

A   10 in

B   10.5 in

C   12 in

D   12.5 in

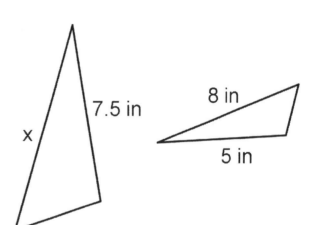

Common Core Standard 7.G.A.1 – Geometry

☐ The drawing below represents a ping-pong table. What is the actual area of the table in real life? Be sure to show your work.

A   2.92 m²

B   2.94 m²

C   2.96 m²

D   2.98 m²

21 cm

14 cm   1 cm = 10 cm

©Teachers' Treasures Publishing

Name_____

ASSESSMENT

Common Core Standard 7.G.A.1 – Geometry

☐ 1 inch on the Texas State map represents an actual distance of 25 miles. The distance between Dallas and Corpus Christi on the map is 14 in. What is the actual distance between the cities? Be sure to show your work.

A   250 miles

B   300 miles

C   350 miles

D   400 miles

Common Core Standard 7.G.A.1 – Geometry

☐ The triangles below are similar. What is the measure of α? Be sure to show your work.

A   20°

B   40°

C   60°

D   80°

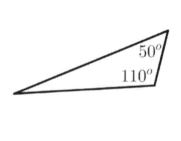

Common Core Standard 7.G.A.1 – Geometry

☐ The drawing below represents an orchard. What is the area of the orchard in real life? Be sure to show your work.

A   648 m²

B   972 m²

C   1,296 m²

D   1,944 m²

18 cm

12 cm   1 cm = 3 m

©Teachers' Treasures Publishing

Name_____

DIAGNOSTIC

Common Core Standard 7.G.A.2 – Geometry

☐ How many triangles can be constructed with the segments in the picture below? Be sure to show your work.

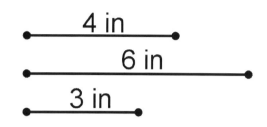

A   0

B   1

C   2

D   infinite number

Common Core Standard 7.G.A.2 – Geometry

☐ How many triangles can be constructed if 2 sides and an angle between them are known? Be sure to show your work.

A   1

B   2

C   3

D   4

Common Core Standard 7.G.A.2 – Geometry

☐ How many triangles can be constructed with angles α=40°, β=50°, γ=90°? Be sure to show your work.

A   0

B   1

C   2

D   infinite number

©Teachers' Treasures Publishing

Name_____

DIAGNOSTIC

Common Core Standard 7.G.A.2 – Geometry

☐ How many triangles can be constructed with the segments and the angle in the picture below, if the angle is between the two sides? Be sure to show your work.

A   0

B   1

C   2

D   infinitely many

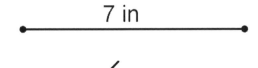

Common Core Standard 7.G.A.2 – Geometry

☐ How many triangles can be constructed if 2 sides and an angle opposite to the shorter side are known? Be sure to show your work.

A   1

B   2

C   3

D   infinite amount

Common Core Standard 7.G.A.2 – Geometry

☐ How many triangles can be constructed with segments with the follwing length: a=11, b=8, c=20? Be sure to show your work.

A   0

B   1

C   2

D   infinite amount

Name_____

PRACTICE

Common Core Standard 7.G.A.2 – Geometry

☐ How many triangles can be constructed with the segments and the angle in the picture below, if the angle is to the opposite of the longer side? Be sure to show your work.

A   0

B   1

C   2

D   infinite amount

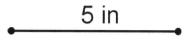
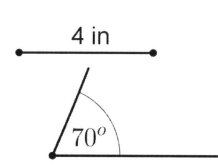

Common Core Standard 7.G.A.2 – Geometry

☐ How many triangles can be constructed if 3 sides are known, where the sum of lengths of any two sides is greater than the length of the remaining side? Be sure to show your work.

A   0

B   1

C   2

D   infinite amount

Common Core Standard 7.G.A.2 – Geometry

☐ How many triangles can be constructed with the following angles: α=35°, β=100°, γ=55°? Be sure to show your work.

A   0

B   1

C   2

D   infinite amount

Name_____

PRACTICE

Common Core Standard 7.G.A.2 – Geometry

☐ How many triangles can be constructed with the segments and the angle in the picture below, if the angle is to the opposite of the shorter side? Be sure to show your work.

A   1

B   2

C   3

D   infinite amount

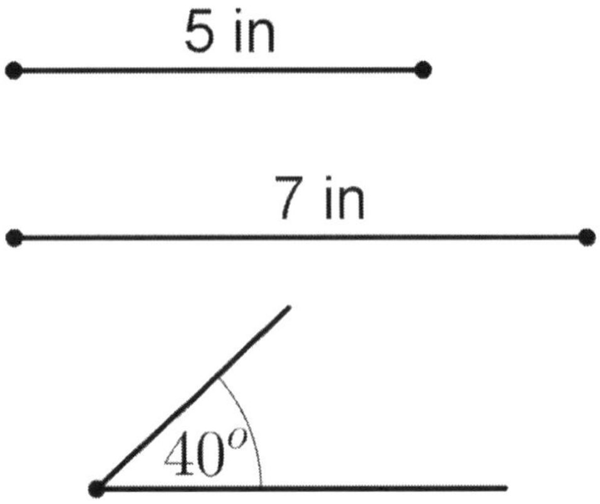

5 in

7 in

40°

Common Core Standard 7.G.A.2 – Geometry

☐ How many triangles can be constructed if 3 sides are known, where one side is longer than the sum of lengths of the remaining two sides? Be sure to show your work.

A   0

B   1

C   2

D   infinite amount

Common Core Standard 7.G.A.2 – Geometry

☐ How many triangles can be constructed with the following segments: a=4, b=6, c=7? Be sure to show your work.

A   0

B   1

C   2

D   infinite amount

Name_____

PRACTICE

Common Core Standard 7.G.A.2 – Geometry

☐ How many triangles can be constructed with the segments in the picture below? Be sure to show your work.

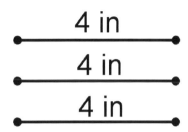

A   0

B   1

C   2

D   infinite amount

Common Core Standard 7.G.A.2 – Geometry

☐ How many triangles can be constructed if 2 sides and an angle opposite to the longer side are known? Be sure to show your work.

A   1

B   2

C   3

D   infinite amount

Common Core Standard 7.G.A.2 – Geometry

☐ How many triangles can be constructed with the following angles: α=65°, β=38°, γ=77°? Be sure to show your work.

A   0

B   1

C   2

D   infinite amount

Name_____

PRACTICE

Common Core Standard 7.G.A.2 – Geometry

☐ How many triangles can be constructed with the segments and the angle in the picture below, if the angle is between the two sides? Be sure to show your work.

A   0

B   1

C   2

D   infinite amount

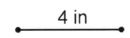
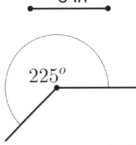

Common Core Standard 7.G.A.2 – Geometry

☐ How many triangles can be constructed with 3 angles, the sum of which is less than 180°? Be sure to show your work.

A   0

B   1

C   2

D   infinite amount

Common Core Standard 7.G.A.2 – Geometry

☐ How many triangles can be constructed with the following segments: a=5, b=14, c=9? Be sure to show your work.

A   0

B   1

C   2

D   infinite amount

Name_____

ASSESSMENT

Common Core Standard 7.G.A.2 – Geometry

☐ How many triangles can be constructed with the segments and the angle in the picture below, if the angle is to the opposite of the shorter side? Be sure to show your work.

A   0
B   1
C   2
D   infinite amount

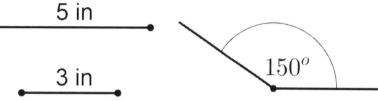

Common Core Standard 7.G.A.2 – Geometry

☐ How many triangles can be constructed with 3 angles the sum of which is greater than 180°? Be sure to show your work.

A   0
B   1
C   2
D   infinite amount

Common Core Standard 7.G.A.2 – Geometry

☐ How many squares can be constructed with a segment the length of which is a=2? Be sure to show your work.

A   0
B   1
C   2
D   infinite amount

©Teachers' Treasures Publishing

Name_____

ASSESSMENT

Common Core Standard 7.G.A.2 – Geometry

How many triangles can be constructed with the segments and the angle in the picture below, if the angle is to the opposite of longer side? Be sure to show your work.

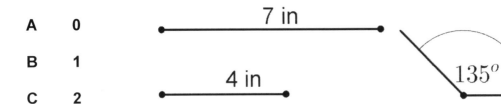

A   0

B   1

C   2

D   infinite amount

Common Core Standard 7.G.A.2 – Geometry

How many triangles can be constructed with 3 angles the sum of which is equal to 180°? Be sure to show your work.

A   0

B   1

C   2

D   infinite amount

Common Core Standard 7.G.A.2 – Geometry

How many squares can be constructed with an angle α=60°? Be sure to show your work.

A   0

B   1

C   2

D   infinite amount

©Teachers' Treasures Publishing

Name_____

DIAGNOSTIC

Common Core Standard 7.G.A.3 – Geometry

☐ What is the intersection of a right square prism and a plane parallel to its base? Be sure to show your work.

A   triangle

B   square

C   rectangle

D   trapezoid

Common Core Standard 7.G.A.3 – Geometry

☐ What is the intersection of a right hexagonal pyramid and a plane parallel to its base? Be sure to show your work.

A   triangle

B   quadrilateral

C   pentagon

D   hexagon

Common Core Standard 7.G.A.3 – Geometry

☐ What may be the intersection of a tetrahedron and a plane parallel to its height? Be sure to show your work.

A   only triangle

B   only quadrilateral

C   triangle or quadrilateral

D   triangle, quadrilateral or pentagon

Name_____

DIAGNOSTIC

Common Core Standard 7.G.A.3 – Geometry

☐ What is the intersection of a right cylinder and a plane parallel to its base? Be sure to show your work.

    A   circle

    B   rectangle

    C   square

    D   triangle

Common Core Standard 7.G.A.3 – Geometry

☐ What may be the intersection of a cube and a plane parallel to its height? Be sure to show your work.

    A   only square

    B   only rectangle

    C   only rhombus

    D   square or rectangle

Common Core Standard 7.G.A.3 – Geometry

☐ What is the intersection of a sphere and a plane? Be sure to show your work.

    A   triangle

    B   circle

    C   square

    D   rectangle

©Teachers' Treasures Publishing

Name_____

PRACTICE

Common Core Standard 7.G.A.3 – Geometry

☐ What may be the intersection of a right square pyramid and a plane parallel to its height? Be sure to show your work.

A   triangle or quadrilateral

B   triangle or circle

C   square or rectangle

D   only square

Common Core Standard 7.G.A.3 – Geometry

☐ What is the intersection of a right cone and a plane parallel to its base? Be sure to show your work.

A   rectangle

B   triangle

C   circle

D   square

Common Core Standard 7.G.A.3 – Geometry

☐ What may be the intersection of a right cylinder and a plane parallel to its height? Be sure to show your work.

A   only circle

B   square or circle

C   circle or rectangle

D   square or rectangle

©Teachers' Treasures Publishing

Name_____

PRACTICE

Common Core Standard 7.G.A.3 – Geometry

☐ **What may be the intersection of a right square prism and a plane parallel to its height? Be sure to show your work.**

A square or rectangle

B only square

C only rhombus

D square or rhombus

Common Core Standard 7.G.A.3 – Geometry

☐ **What is the intersection of a cube and a plane parallel to its base? Be sure to show your work.**

A triangle

B square

C rectangle

D trapezoid

Common Core Standard 7.G.A.3 – Geometry

☐ **What is the intersection of a right cone and a plane which contains its height? Be sure to show your work.**

A triangle

B circle

C square

D rectangle

Name_____

PRACTICE

Common Core Standard 7.G.A.3 – Geometry

☐ What is the intersection of a right rectangular prism and a plane parallel to its height? Be sure to show your work.

    A   rectangle

    B   rhombus

    C   trapezoid

    D   triangle

Common Core Standard 7.G.A.3 – Geometry

☐ What is the intersection of a right hexagonal prism and a plane parallel to its base? Be sure to show your work.

    A   triangle

    B   rectangle

    C   pentagon

    D   hexagon

Common Core Standard 7.G.A.3 – Geometry

☐ What is the intersection of a tetrahedron and a plane parallel to its base? Be sure to show your work.

    A   triangle

    B   rectangle

    C   pentagon

    D   hexagon

©Teachers' Treasures Publishing

Name_____

PRACTICE

Common Core Standard 7.G.A.3 – Geometry

☐ Which of the following cannot be the intersection of a plane and a right cylinder? Be sure to show your work.

    A   circle

    B   triangle

    C   rectangle

    D   square

Common Core Standard 7.G.A.3 – Geometry

☐ What is the intersection of a right square pyramid and a plane parallel to its base? Be sure to show your work.

    A   triangle

    B   rectangle

    C   square

    D   trapezoid

Common Core Standard 7.G.A.3 – Geometry

☐ What is the intersection of a right hexagonal pyramid and a plane which contains its height? Be sure to show your work.

    A   triangle

    B   rectangle

    C   pentagon

    D   hexagon

©Teachers' Treasures Publishing

Name_____

ASSESSMENT

Common Core Standard 7.G.A.3 – Geometry

☐ Which of the following cannot be the intersection of a plane and a right cone? Be sure to show your work.

A square

B triangle

C circle

D ellipse

Common Core Standard 7.G.A.3 – Geometry

☐ What is the intersection of a right triangular pyramid and a plane parallel to its base? Be sure to show your work.

A triangle

B square

C rectangle

D rhombus

Common Core Standard 7.G.A.3 – Geometry

☐ What is the intersection of a right rectangular prism and a plane parallel to its base? Be sure to show your work.

A triangle

B square

C rectangle

D trapezoid

Name_____

ASSESSMENT

Common Core Standard 7.G.A.3 – Geometry

☐ Which of the following cannot be the intersection of a plane and a cube? Be sure to show your work.

  A   triangle

  B   square

  C   rectangle

  D   circle

Common Core Standard 7.G.A.3 – Geometry

☐ What is the intersection of a right hexagonal prism and a plane parallel to its height? Be sure to show your work.

  A   triangle

  B   rectangle

  C   pentagon

  D   hexagon

Common Core Standard 7.G.A.3 – Geometry

☐ What is the intersection of a right triangular prism and a plane parallel to its base? Be sure to show your work.

  A   triangle

  B   rectangle

  C   square

  D   pentagon

©Teachers' Treasures Publishing

Name_____

DIAGNOSTIC

Common Core Standard 7.G.B.4 – Geometry

☐ The diameter of a circular sumo wrestling ring is 14.9 ft. What is the area of the sumo wrestling ring? Be sure to show your work.

A 174.28 ft²

B 174.63 ft²

C 175.37 ft²

D 175.63 ft²

Common Core Standard 7.G.B.4 – Geometry

☐ What is the circumference of a circle if the radius of the circle is 6 in? Be sure to show your work.

A 3π in

B 6π in

C 12π in

D 36π in

Common Core Standard 7.G.B.4 – Geometry

☐ The radius of a bicycle wheel is 20 cm. What is the circumference of the bicycle wheel? Be sure to show your work.

A 10π cm

B 20π cm

C 30π cm

D 40π cm

Name_____

DIAGNOSTIC

Common Core Standard 7.G.B.4 – Geometry

☐ The radio station has a broadcasting radius of 40 miles. What area does the radio station cover? Be sure to show your work.

A 40π mi^2

B 80π mi^2

C 400π mi^2

D $1{,}600\pi$ mi^2

Common Core Standard 7.G.B.4 – Geometry

☐ What is the area of a circle if the radius of the circle is 8? Be sure to show your work.

A 16π

B 64π

C 128π

D 256π

Common Core Standard 7.G.B.4 – Geometry

☐ What is the circumference of a hotplate if the diameter of the hotplate is 18 cm? Be sure to show your work.

A 18π cm

B 36π cm

C 54π cm

D 72π cm

Name _____

PRACTICE

Common Core Standard 7.G.B.4 – Geometry

☐ What is the circumference of a hat if the diameter measures 24 cm? Be sure to show your work.

A 12π cm

B 24π cm

C 36π cm

D 48π cm

Common Core Standard 7.G.B.4 – Geometry

☐ What is the area of a circle given the circumference is 12π? Be sure to show your work.

A 36π

B 72π

C 144π

D 288π

Common Core Standard 7.G.B.4 – Geometry

☐ A dog is tied with a leash that has a length of 2 m. What is the area in which dog can move? Be sure to show your work.

A 4π m^2

B 16π m^2

C 64π m^2

D 256π m^2

Name_____

PRACTICE

Common Core Standard 7.G.B.4 – Geometry

☐ The circumference of the Earth's equator is 40,000 km. What is the best estimate of the radius of Earth? Be sure to show your work.

- A 4,400 km
- B 5,400 km
- C 6,400 km
- D 7,400 km

Common Core Standard 7.G.B.4 – Geometry

☐ What is the circumference of a circle when the area of the circle measures 144π? Be sure to show your work.

- A 12π
- B 24π
- C 36π
- D 48π

Common Core Standard 7.G.B.4 – Geometry

☐ The area of a traffic sign measures 81π in². What is its' radius? Be sure to show your work.

- A 3 in
- B 6 in
- C 9 in
- D 12 in

Name _____

PRACTICE

Common Core Standard 7.G.B.4 – Geometry

☐ **What is the area of a badge if the diameter of the badge measures 2 in? Be sure to show your work.**

    A   π in²

    B   2π in²

    C   3π in²

    D   4π in²

Common Core Standard 7.G.B.4 – Geometry

☐ **What is the radius of a circle when the circumference of the circle measures 6π in²? Be sure to show your work.**

    A   3 in

    B   6 in

    C   9 in

    D   12 in

Common Core Standard 7.G.B.4 – Geometry

☐ **What is the circumference of a basketball rim if its diameter is 18 in? Be sure to show your work.**

    A   9π in

    B   18π in

    C   36π in

    D   81π in

©Teachers' Treasures Publishing

Name_____

PRACTICE

Common Core Standard 7.G.B.4 – Geometry

☐ **An old music record has an area of 625π cm². What is the radius of the disk? Be sure to show your work.**

A   15 cm

B   20 cm

C   25 cm

D   30 cm

Common Core Standard 7.G.B.4 – Geometry

☐ **What is the radius of a circle when the area of the circle measures 64π? Be sure to show your work.**

A   4

B   8

C   16

D   32

Common Core Standard 7.G.B.4 – Geometry

☐ **What is the circumference of a flowerpot if the diameter at the top measures 8 in? Be sure to show your work.**

A   4π in

B   8π in

C   16π in

D   32π in

Name_____

ASSESSMENT

Common Core Standard 7.G.B.4 – Geometry

☐ **A compact disc has a circumference of 12π cm. What is the radius of the disc? Be sure to show your work.**

A   6 cm

B   12 cm

C   18 cm

D   24 cm

Common Core Standard 7.G.B.4 – Geometry

☐ **What is the radius of a circle that has equal area and circumference? Be sure to show your work.**

A   1

B   2

C   π

D   2π

Common Core Standard 7.G.B.4 – Geometry

☐ **What is the radius of the base of a pot when the area of the pot measures 49π in^2? Be sure to show your work.**

A   4 in

B   7 in

C   9 in

D   14 in

©Teachers' Treasures Publishing

Name _____

ASSESSMENT

Common Core Standard 7.G.B.4 – Geometry

☐ What is the diameter of a tire when given the circumference of the tire measures 32π in? Be sure to show your work.

A   8 in

B   16 in

C   32 in

D   64 in

Common Core Standard 7.G.B.4 – Geometry

☐ What is the radius of a circle if the circumference measures twice as much as its area? Be sure to show your work.

A   1

B   2

C   π

D   2π

Common Core Standard 7.G.B.4 – Geometry

☐ What is the circumference of a cup when give the diameter of the cup measures 8 cm? Be sure to show your work.

A   2π cm

B   4π cm

C   8π cm

D   16π cm

©Teachers' Treasures Publishing

Name_____   DIAGNOSTIC

Common Core Standard 7.G.B.5 – Geometry

☐ The angles in the picture below are complementary. What is the measure of α? Be sure to show your work.

A   38°

B   48°

C   52°

D   128°

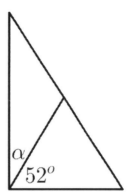

Common Core Standard 7.G.B.5 – Geometry

☐ What is the sum of two supplementary angles? Be sure to show your work.

A   90°

B   180°

C   270°

D   360°

Common Core Standard 7.G.B.5 – Geometry

☐ What is the measure of α in the picture below? Be sure to show your work.

A   8°

B   18°

C   82°

D   98°

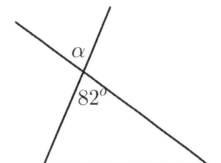

©Teachers' Treasures Publishing

Name_____

DIAGNOSTIC

Common Core Standard 7.G.B.5 – Geometry

☐   What is the measure of α in the picture below? Be sure to show your work.

A   32°

B   46°

C   78°

D   110°

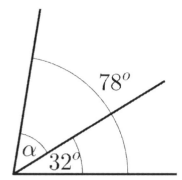

Common Core Standard 7.G.B.5 – Geometry

☐   What is the sum of two complementary angles? Be sure to show your work.

A   90°

B   180°

C   270°

D   360°

Common Core Standard 7.G.B.5 – Geometry

☐   What is the measure of α in the picture below? Be sure to show your work.

A   35°

B   55°

C   135°

D   155°

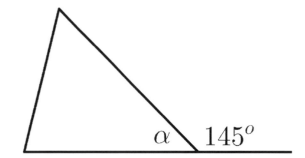

©Teachers' Treasures Publishing

Name_____

PRACTICE

Common Core Standard 7.G.B.5 – Geometry

☐ The angles in the picture below are complementary. What is the measure of α? Be sure to show your work.

A   9°

B   12°

C   18°

D   36°

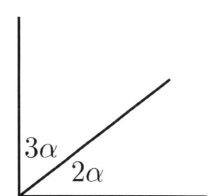

Common Core Standard 7.G.B.5 – Geometry

☐ If α=40°, and α and β are vertical angles, what is the value of β? Be sure to show your work.

A   40°

B   50°

C   140°

D   150°

Common Core Standard 7.G.B.5 – Geometry

☐ What is the measure of α in the picture below? Be sure to show your work.

A   42°

B   48°

C   58°

D   142°

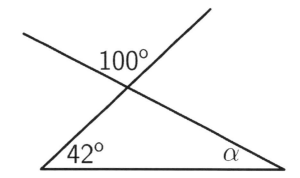

©Teachers' Treasures Publishing

Name_____

PRACTICE

Common Core Standard 7.G.B.5 – Geometry

What is the measure of α in the picture below? Be sure to show your work.

A   5°

B   10°

C   15°

D   20°

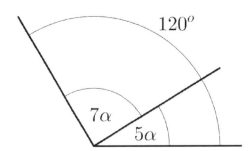

Common Core Standard 7.G.B.5 – Geometry

How many common vertices do two adjacent angles have? Be sure to show your work.

A   0

B   1

C   2

D   3

Common Core Standard 7.G.B.5 – Geometry

What is the measure of α in the picture below? Be sure to show your work.

A   15°

B   20°

C   25°

D   30°

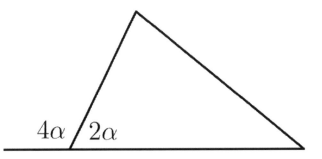

©Teachers' Treasures Publishing

Name_____

PRACTICE

Common Core Standard 7.G.B.5 – Geometry

☐ What is the measure of α in the picture below? Be sure to show your work.

A   39°
B   49°
C   51°
D   129°

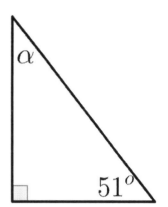

Common Core Standard 7.G.B.5 – Geometry

☐ Which angle in the picture below is supplementary to θ? Be sure to show your work.

A   α
B   β
C   γ
D   δ

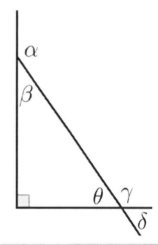

Common Core Standard 7.G.B.5 – Geometry

☐ What is the measure of α in the picture below? Be sure to show your work.

A   8°
B   12°
C   16°
D   20°

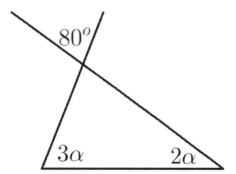

©Teachers' Treasures Publishing

Name_____

PRACTICE

Common Core Standard 7.G.B.5 – Geometry

☐ What is the measure of α in the picture below? Be sure to show your work.

A   35°

B   40°

C   45°

D   60°

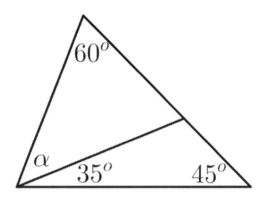

Common Core Standard 7.G.B.5 – Geometry

☐ Which angle in the picture below is complementary to θ? Be sure to show your work.

A   α

B   β

C   γ

D   δ

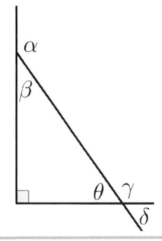

Common Core Standard 7.G.B.5 – Geometry

☐ The difference of two supplementary angles is 40°. What is the measure of greater angle? Be sure to show your work.

A   65°

B   70°

C   110°

D   140°

©Teachers' Treasures Publishing

Name_____

ASSESSMENT

Common Core Standard 7.G.B.5 – Geometry

☐ What is the measure of α in the picture below? Be sure to show your work.

A   4°

B   5°

C   9°

D   10°

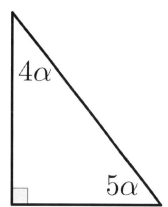

Common Core Standard 7.G.B.5 – Geometry

☐ Which angle in the picture below is vertical to θ? Be sure to show your work.

A   α

B   β

C   γ

D   δ

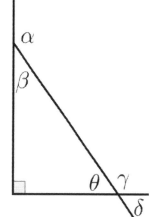

Common Core Standard 7.G.B.5 – Geometry

☐ What is the measure of α in the picture below? Be sure to show your work.

A   10°

B   15°

C   20°

D   25°

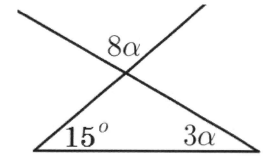

©Teachers' Treasures Publishing

Name_____

ASSESSMENT

Common Core Standard 7.G.B.5 – Geometry

What is the measure of α in the picture below? Be sure to show your work.

A 5°

B 10°

C 15°

D 20°

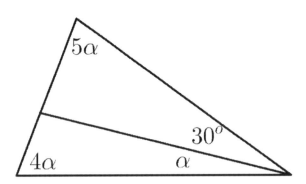

Common Core Standard 7.G.B.5 – Geometry

Which angle in the picture below is adjacent to θ? Be sure to show your work.

A α

B β

C γ

D δ

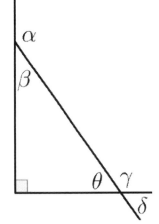

Common Core Standard 7.G.B.5 – Geometry

The difference of two complementary angles is 40°. What is the measure of the greater angle? Be sure to show your work.

A 45°

B 65°

C 70°

D 110°

©Teachers' Treasures Publishing

Name_____

DIAGNOSTIC

Common Core Standard 7.G.B.6 – Geometry

☐ **What is the area of a tile the width of which is 8 in and length is 12 in? Be sure to show your work.**

A   20 in^2

B   40 in^2

C   48 in^2

D   96 in^2

Common Core Standard 7.G.B.6 – Geometry

☐ **What is the volume of a cube the edge of which is 5 in long? Be sure to show your work.**

A   5 in^3

B   10 in^3

C   25 in^3

D   125 in^3

Common Core Standard 7.G.B.6 – Geometry

☐ **What is the surface area of a matchbox the length of which is 3 in, width is 2 in, and height is 1 in? Be sure to show your work.**

A   6 in^2

B   11 in^2

C   22 in^2

D   33 in^2

Name_____

DIAGNOSTIC

Common Core Standard 7.G.B.6 – Geometry

☐ **What is the surface area of a Rubik's Cube the edge of which is 3 in? Be sure to show your work.**

- A   27 in^2
- B   54 in^2
- C   81 in^2
- D   108 in^2

Common Core Standard 7.G.B.6 – Geometry

☐ **What is the area of a rectangle the length of which is 12 in and the width is 7 in? Be sure to show your work.**

- A   5 in^2
- B   19 in^2
- C   84 in^2
- D   127 in^2

Common Core Standard 7.G.B.6 – Geometry

☐ **What is the volume of an aquarium that is 3 ft long, 1 ft wide, and 2 ft high? Be sure to show your work.**

- A   6 ft^3
- B   11 ft^3
- C   22 ft^3
- D   312 ft^3

Name_____

PRACTICE

Common Core Standard 7.G.B.6 – Geometry

☐ **What is the volume of a milk jug with the following dimensions: base is 3 in by 3 in, and height is 12 in? Be sure to show your work.**

    A   108 in^3

    B   72 in^3

    C   45 in^3

    D   18 in^3

Common Core Standard 7.G.B.6 – Geometry

☐ **What is the surface area of a right rectangular prism the dimensions of which are 4 in, 6 in, and 10 in? Be sure to show your work.**

    A   248 in^2

    B   240 in^2

    C   124 in^2

    D   100 in^2

Common Core Standard 7.G.B.6 – Geometry

☐ **What is the area of a painting the dimensions of which are 3 ft and 2 ft? Be sure to show your work.**

    A   5 ft^2

    B   6 ft^2

    C   23 ft^2

    D   32 ft^2

©Teachers' Treasures Publishing

Name_____

PRACTICE

Common Core Standard 7.G.B.6 – Geometry

☐ What is the area of a floor rug the width of which is 4 yd and the length is 6 yd? Be sure to show your work.

  A 10 yd^2

  B 24 yd^2

  C 46 yd^2

  D 64 yd^2

Common Core Standard 7.G.B.6 – Geometry

☐ What is the volume of a square prism that is 4 in wide and 8 in high? Be sure to show your work.

  A 32 in^3

  B 48 in^3

  C 84 in^3

  D 128 in^3

Common Core Standard 7.G.B.6 – Geometry

☐ What is the surface area of a brick the dimensions of which are 3 in, 8 in, and 4 in? Be sure to show your work.

  A 68 in^2

  B 96 in^2

  C 136 in^2

  D 384 in^2

©Teachers' Treasures Publishing

Name_____

PRACTICE

Common Core Standard 7.G.B.6 – Geometry

☐ **What is the surface area of an ice cube with 1 in edge? Be sure to show your work.**

    A   1 in^2

    B   4 in^2

    C   6 in^2

    D   11 in^2

Common Core Standard 7.G.B.6 – Geometry

☐ **What is the area of a right triangle the catheti of which are 4 in and 6 in? Be sure to show your work.**

    A   5 in^2

    B   10 in^2

    C   12 in^2

    D   24 in^2

Common Core Standard 7.G.B.6 – Geometry

☐ **What is the volume of a swimming pool that is 10 m wide, 20 m long, and 2 m deep? Be sure to show your work.**

    A   200 m^3

    B   260 m^3

    C   400 m^3

    D   520 m^3

©Teachers' Treasures Publishing

Name_____

PRACTICE

Common Core Standard 7.G.B.6 – Geometry

☐ What is the volume of an ark the width of which is 2 ft, the length is 4 ft, and the height is 2 ft? Be sure to show your work.

- A   8 ft^3
- B   16 ft^3
- C   20 ft^3
- D   40 ft^3

Common Core Standard 7.G.B.6 – Geometry

☐ What is the surface area of a tetrahedron with a 3 in edge? Be sure to show your work.

- A   3 in^2
- B   3$\sqrt{3}$ in^2
- C   9 in^2
- D   9$\sqrt{3}$ in^2

Common Core Standard 7.G.B.6 – Geometry

☐ What is the area of an envelope the dimensions of which are 4 in and 9 in? Be sure to show your work.

- A   13 in^2
- B   18 in^2
- C   26 in^2
- D   36 in^2

©Teachers' Treasures Publishing

Name_____

ASSESSMENT

Common Core Standard 7.G.B.6 – Geometry

☐ What is the area of a photo ID the dimensions of which are 4 in and 7 in? Be sure to show your work.

- A   11 in²
- B   28 in²
- C   47 in²
- D   74 in²

Common Core Standard 7.G.B.6 – Geometry

☐ What is the volume of a cube the surface area of which is 96 in²? Be sure to show your work.

- A   8 in³
- B   16 in³
- C   32 in³
- D   64 in³

Common Core Standard 7.G.B.6 – Geometry

☐ What is the surface area of a cube box the edge of which is 8 in? Be sure to show your work.

- A   64 in²
- B   216 in²
- C   384 in²
- D   512 in²

©Teachers' Treasures Publishing

Name_____

ASSESSMENT

Common Core Standard 7.G.B.6 – Geometry

☐ What is the surface area of a refrigerator with the following dimensions: the base is 2 ft by 2 ft, and the height is 6 ft? Be sure to show your work.

  A   24 ft²

  B   28 ft²

  C   56 ft²

  D   226 ft²

Common Core Standard 7.G.B.6 – Geometry

☐ What is the side of a square with an equal area and perimeter? Be sure to show your work.

  A   4

  B   5

  C   6

  D   7

Common Core Standard 7.G.B.6 – Geometry

☐ What is the volume of a locker the dimensions of which are 1 ft, 2 ft, and 5 ft? Be sure to show your work.

  A   10 ft³

  B   17 ft³

  C   34 ft³

  D   125 ft³

©Teachers' Treasures Publishing

Name_____

DIAGNOSTIC

Common Core Standard 7.SP.A.1 – Statistics & Probability

☐ Kimberly polled the 3 tallest students of her class. Is this sample of students likely to be biased? Explain your answer.

A   yes

B   no

C   yes, if she polled dark haired students

D   it is not possible to conclude

Common Core Standard 7.SP.A.1 – Statistics & Probability

☐ 4 of the classes have the same number of students. The teacher selected 2 students from each class. Is this sample of students likely to be random? Explain your answer.

A   yes

B   no

C   yes, if he polled female students

D   it is not possible to conclude

Common Core Standard 7.SP.A.1 – Statistics & Probability

☐ Zoey surveyed 10 of the wealthiest citizens in the state. Is this sample of citizens likely to be representative? Explain your answer.

A   yes, if he polled men

B   no

C   yes

D   it is not possible to conclude

Common Core Standard 7.SP.A.1 – Statistics & Probability

☐   Sadie polled the 3 oldest neighbors. Is this sample of neighbors likely to be biased? Explain your answer.

    A   yes, if she polled women

    B   no

    C   yes

    D   it is not possible to conclude

Common Core Standard 7.SP.A.1 – Statistics & Probability

☐   4 bags have an equal number of apples. Wyatt selected 3 apples from each bag. Is this sample of apples likely to be random? Explain your answer.

    A   yes, if he selected red apples

    B   no

    C   yes

    D   it is not possible to conclude

Common Core Standard 7.SP.A.1 – Statistics & Probability

☐   Emma surveyed only female employees in the company. Is this sample of employees likely to be representative?   Explain your answer.

    A   yes, if the number of females and males is equal

    B   no

    C   yes

    D   it is not possible to conclude

Name_____

PRACTICE

Common Core Standard 7.SP.A.1 – Statistics & Probability

☐ Landon selected 2 bottles of mineral water from the pack of 50 identical bottles. Is this sample of bottles likely to be biased? Explain your answer.

A   yes, if he selected bottles of 2 liters

B   no

C   yes

D   it is not possible to conclude

Common Core Standard 7.SP.A.1 – Statistics & Probability

☐ 5 storage boxes contain different number of toys. Alexa selected 2 toys from each box. Is this sample of toys likely to be random? Explain your answer.

A   yes, if she selected dolls

B   yes

C   no

D   it is not possible to conclude

Common Core Standard 7.SP.A.1 – Statistics & Probability

☐ Samuel surveyed only employees with green eyes at XYZ Company. Is this sample of employees likely to be representative? Explain your answer.

A   no

B   yes

C   yes, if the number of females and males in the company is equal

D   it is not possible to conclude

©Teachers' Treasures Publishing

Name_____

PRACTICE

Common Core Standard 7.SP.A.1 – Statistics & Probability

☐ Lauren selected 3 bulbs from a pack of 200 identical bulbs. Is this sample of bulbs likely to be biased? Explain your answer.

    A   yes, if she selected bulbs of 60 Watts

    B   no

    C   yes

    D   it is not possible to conclude

Common Core Standard 7.SP.A.1 – Statistics & Probability

☐ 6 packages contain an equal number of nails. Aaron selected 5 nails from each package. Is this sample of nails likely to be random? Explain your answer.

    A   yes

    B   no, if he selected nails 5 inches long

    C   no

    D   it is not possible to conclude

Common Core Standard 7.SP.A.1 – Statistics & Probability

☐ Chase surveyed only divorced males at the movie theater snack stand. Is this sample of people at the theater likely to be representative?   Explain your answer.

    A   no

    B   yes

    C   yes, if the number of females and males visitors is equal

    D   it is not possible to conclude

Name_____

PRACTICE

Common Core Standard 7.SP.A.1 – Statistics & Probability

☐ **Nicholas selected 3 shirts from the rack of 500 identical shirts. Is this sample of shirts likely to be biased? Explain your answer.**

A   no

B   yes, if he selected blue shirts

C   yes

D   it is not possible to conclude

Common Core Standard 7.SP.A.1 – Statistics & Probability

☐ **4 plastic boxes contain an equal number of marbles. Lydia selected 4 marbles from the first 2 packages. Is this sample of marbles likely to be random? Explain your answer.**

A   yes

B   yes, if she selected green marbles

C   no

D   it is not possible to conclude

Common Core Standard 7.SP.A.1 – Statistics & Probability

☐ **Quinn surveyed the first 5 people who visited the toy store. Is this sample of visitors of the toy store likely to be representative? Explain your answer.**

A   no

B   yes

C   yes, if the total number of visitors is less than 100

D   it is not possible to conclude

©Teachers' Treasures Publishing

Name_____

PRACTICE

Common Core Standard 7.SP.A.1 – Statistics & Probability

☐ **Izabella selected 3 of the oldest cars from the parking lot. Is this sample of cars on the parking lot is likely to be biased? Explain your answer.**

- A no
- B yes, if she selected red cars
- C yes
- D it is not possible to conclude

Common Core Standard 7.SP.A.1 – Statistics & Probability

☐ **5 bags contain an equal number of rocks. Emmett selected 3 rocks from each of the packages. Is this sample of rocks likely to be random? Be sure to show your work.**

- A yes
- B yes, if she selected red marbles
- C no
- D it is not possible to conclude

Common Core Standard 7.SP.A.1 – Statistics & Probability

☐ **Hayden surveyed the last 4 people who entered the bus station. Is this sample of passengers is likely to be representative? Explain your answer.**

- A no
- B yes
- C yes, if the total number of passengers is less than 50
- D it is not possible to conclude

©Teachers' Treasures Publishing

Name_____

ASSESSMENT

Common Core Standard 7.SP.A.1 – Statistics & Probability

☐ Kingston selected 3 kangaroos from the zoo. Is this sample of animals at the zoo likely to be biased? Explain your answer.

A   no

B   no, if she selected kangaroos from Australia

C   yes

D   it is not possible to conclude

Common Core Standard 7.SP.A.1 – Statistics & Probability

☐ 5 baskets contain an equal number of pears. Jameson selected 5 pears from the first 3 baskets and 3 pears from the last 2 baskets. Is this sample of pears likely to be random? Explain your answer.

A   yes, if he selected yellow pears

B   yes

C   no

D   it is not possible to conclude

Common Core Standard 7.SP.A.1 – Statistics & Probability

☐ Mckenna surveyed 5 voters who were younger than 25 years. Is this sample of voters likely to be representative? Explain your answer.

A   no

B   yes, if the total number of voters is less than 100

C   yes

D   it is not possible to conclude

©Teachers' Treasures Publishing

Name_____

ASSESSMENT

Common Core Standard 7.SP.A.1 – Statistics & Probability

☐ The teacher selected 3 boys from the class with an equal number of boys and girls. Is this sample of students likely to be biased? Explain your answer.

A   no

B   yes

C   no, if teacher selected students with good behavior

D   it is not possible to conclude

Common Core Standard 7.SP.A.1 – Statistics & Probability

☐ A policeman stopped 5 cars with an equal number of passengers. The policeman selected 1 passenger from each car for an alcohol test. Is this sample of passengers likely to be random? Explain your answer.

A   yes, if selected passengers are women

B   yes

C   no

D   it is not possible to conclude

Common Core Standard 7.SP.A.1 – Statistics & Probability

☐ Omar surveyed 5 football players older than 30 years. Is this sample of football players likely to be representative? Explain your answer.

A   no

B   yes, if the football players are American citizens

C   yes

D   it is not possible to conclude

©Teachers' Treasures Publishing

Name_____

DIAGNOSTIC

Common Core Standard 7.SP.A.2 – Statistics & Probability

☐ **A promoter of a rock concert distributed 72 yellow shirts to the visitors. Later during the concert, the promoter counted 8 visitors in those yellow shirts from a group of 1,000 visitors. Estimate the number of visitors of the rock concert. Be sure to show your work.**

A 7,000

B 8,000

C 9,000

D 10,000

Common Core Standard 7.SP.A.2 – Statistics & Probability

☐ **Corbin polled 50 people at the football game. 6 of them were women. If the total number of viewers at the football game was 6,000, estimate the number of women. Be sure to show your work.**

A 620

B 720

C 820

D 920

Common Core Standard 7.SP.A.2 – Statistics & Probability

☐ **3 out of 5 polled students are boys. The total number of students is 1,200. Estimate the number of boys. Be sure to show your work.**

A 480

B 580

C 620

D 720

Name_____

DIAGNOSTIC

Common Core Standard 7.SP.A.2 – Statistics & Probability

☐ **Devin tagged 65 fish in the lake. Later he counted 13 tagged fish from the school of 800 fish. Estimate the number of fish in the lake. Be sure to show your work.**

A 4,000

B 5,000

C 6,000

D 7,000

Common Core Standard 7.SP.A.2 – Statistics & Probability

☐ **Jada polled 20 people at the art exhibition. 3 of them said they will visit the art exhibition again. If the number of visitors at the art exhibition was 500, estimate the number of people who will come again. Be sure to show your work.**

A 70

B 75

C 80

D 85

Common Core Standard 7.SP.A.2 – Statistics & Probability

☐ **2 out of 15 polled students take Spanish as a second language. The total number of students who take Spanish is 46. Estimate the number of students. Be sure to show your work.**

A 345

B 445

C 545

D 645

Name_____

PRACTICE

Common Core Standard 7.SP.A.2 – Statistics & Probability

☐ **Lorenzo tagged 36 baboons at the wild life preservation. Later he counted 4 tagged baboons from the troop of 23 baboons. Estimate the number of baboons at the preservation. Be sure to show your work.**

- A 100
- B 150
- C 200
- D 250

Common Core Standard 7.SP.A.2 – Statistics & Probability

☐ **Kaydence polled 30 people at the theater. 9 of them had membership and go to a play every week. If the number of visitors was 400, estimate the number of people who go to theater every week. Be sure to show your work.**

- A 80
- B 100
- C 120
- D 140

Common Core Standard 7.SP.A.2 – Statistics & Probability

☐ **7 out of 20 polled tourists who stayed at the hotel were teenagers. The total number of teenagers at the hotel was 35. Estimate the number of tourists staying at the hotel. Be sure to show your work.**

- A 100
- B 200
- C 300
- D 400

Name_____

PRACTICE

Common Core Standard 7.SP.A.2 – Statistics & Probability

☐ **Jeffrey tagged 15 hawks at a national park. Later he counted 6 tagged hawks from the flock of 25 hawks. Estimate the number of hawks at the national park. Be sure to show your work.**

    A   50

    B   60

    C   70

    D   80

Common Core Standard 7.SP.A.2 – Statistics & Probability

☐ **Teagan polled 25 people at the party. 11 of them were drinking soda. If the total number of people at the party was 200, estimate the number of people who were drinking soda at the party. Be sure to show your work.**

    A   70

    B   80

    C   90

    D   100

Common Core Standard 7.SP.A.2 – Statistics & Probability

☐ **7 out of 15 polled voters were younger than 30 years. The total number of voters younger than 30 years was 70. Estimate the number of voters. Be sure to show your work.**

    A   100

    B   150

    C   200

    D   250

©Teachers' Treasures Publishing

Name_____

PRACTICE

Common Core Standard 7.SP.A.2 – Statistics & Probability

☐ **Eloise tagged 20 cows on the farm. Later she counted 9 tagged cows from the herd of 63 cows. Estimate the number of cows on the farm. Be sure to show your work.**

    A   120

    B   140

    C   160

    D   180

Common Core Standard 7.SP.A.2 – Statistics & Probability

☐ **Alex polled 22 people at a basketball game. 6 of them were eating snacks. If the number of viewers at the basketball game was 1,500, estimate the number of people who were eating snacks. Be sure to show your work.**

    A   200

    B   300

    C   400

    D   500

Common Core Standard 7.SP.A.2 – Statistics & Probability

☐ **4 out of 25 polled teachers use public transportation. The total number of teachers in the town is 700. Estimate the number of teachers who use public transportation. Be sure to show your work.**

    A   100

    B   200

    C   300

    D   400

Name_____

PRACTICE

Common Core Standard 7.SP.A.2 – Statistics & Probability

☐ Walker tagged 30 chickens on the farm. Later he counted 7 tagged chickens from the flock of 40 chickens. Estimate the number of chickens on the farm. Be sure to show your work.

　　A　130

　　B　150

　　C　170

　　D　190

Common Core Standard 7.SP.A.2 – Statistics & Probability

☐ Rosalie polled 18 employees at a company meeting. 6 of them were satisfied with their salary. If the number of employees at the meeting was 150, estimate the number of employees who were satisfied with their salary. Be sure to show your work.

　　A　20

　　B　30

　　C　40

　　D　50

Common Core Standard 7.SP.A.2 – Statistics & Probability

☐ 4 out of 7 polled teachers use the computer room. The total number of teachers who use the computer room in the school is 60. Estimate the number of teachers in the school. Be sure to show your work.

　　A　70

　　B　80

　　C　90

　　D　100

Name_____

ASSESSMENT

Common Core Standard 7.SP.A.2 – Statistics & Probability

☐ Tate tagged 20 pigeons in the cage. Later he counted 4 tagged pigeons from the flock of 80 pigeons. Estimate the number of pigeons. Be sure to show your work.

    A   300

    B   400

    C   500

    D   600

Common Core Standard 7.SP.A.2 – Statistics & Probability

☐ Lucille polled 25 basketball players at the tournament. 8 of them were older than 30 years. If the number of players older than 30 years at the tournament was 32, estimate the total number of players. Be sure to show your work.

    A   100

    B   150

    C   200

    D   250

Common Core Standard 7.SP.A.2 – Statistics & Probability

☐ 3 out of 8 polled students play basketball. The total number of students is 1,120. Estimate the number of students who play basketball. Be sure to show your work.

    A   360

    B   380

    C   400

    D   420

©Teachers' Treasures Publishing

Name_____

ASSESSMENT

Common Core Standard 7.SP.A.2 – Statistics & Probability

☐ **Scarlett tagged 13 penguins on the beach. Later she counted 3 tagged penguins from the flock of 70 penguins. Estimate the number of penguins. Be sure to show your work.**

    A   300

    B   400

    C   500

    D   600

Common Core Standard 7.SP.A.2 – Statistics & Probability

☐ **Samuel polled 30 buyers at the bakery. 23 of them buy bread from the bakery every day. If the total number of buyers was 270, estimate the number of buyers who buy bread every day. Be sure to show your work.**

    A   100

    B   150

    C   200

    D   250

Common Core Standard 7.SP.A.2 – Statistics & Probability

☐ **2 out of 25 polled bus drivers are women. The total number of bus drivers is 500. Estimate the number of female bus drivers. Be sure to show your work.**

    A   25

    B   30

    C   35

    D   40

©Teachers' Treasures Publishing

Name_____

Common Core Standard 7.SP.B.3 – Statistics & Probability

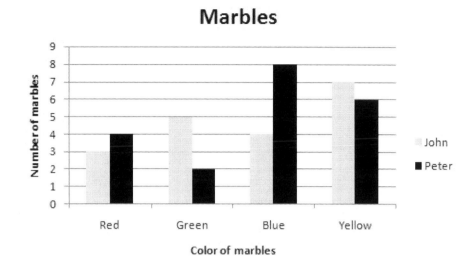

☐ Look at the graph above. How many more marbles does Peter have than John?

A   1   C   3

B   2   D   4

Common Core Standard 7.SP.B.3 – Statistics & Probability

☐ What is the difference between the mean values of Peter's and John's marbles?

A   0   C   0.5

B   0.25   D   0.75

Common Core Standard 7.SP.B.3 – Statistics & Probability

☐ What is the difference between the mean absolute deviations of Peter's and John's marbles?

A   0   C   0.5

B   0.25   D   0.75

Name_____

DIAGNOSTIC

Common Core Standard 7.SP.B.3 – Statistics & Probability

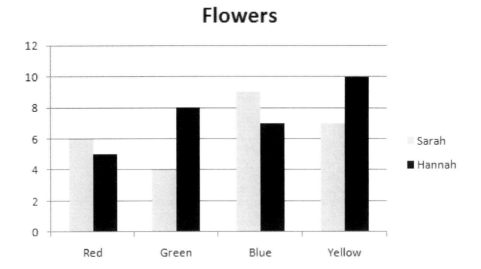

☐ Look at the graph above. How many more flowers does Hannah have than Sarah?

A   1   C   3

B   2   D   4

Common Core Standard 7.SP.B.3 – Statistics & Probability

☐ What is the difference between the mean values of Hannah's and Sarah's flowers?

A   0   C   2

B   1   D   3

Common Core Standard 7.SP.B.3 – Statistics & Probability

☐ What is the difference between the mean absolute deviations of Hannah's and Sarah's flowers?

A   0   C   0.5

B   0.25   D   0.75

©Teachers' Treasures Publishing

Name_____

PRACTICE

Common Core Standard 7.SP.B.3 – Statistics & Probability

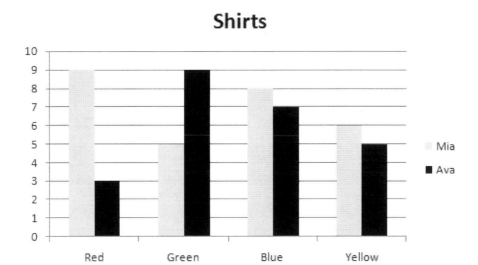

☐ Look at the graph above. How many more shirts does Mia have than Ava?

A   1   C   3

B   2   D   4

Common Core Standard 7.SP.B.3 – Statistics & Probability

☐ What is the difference between the mean values of Mia's and Ava's shirts?

A   0   C   1

B   0.5   D   1.5

Common Core Standard 7.SP.B.3 – Statistics & Probability

☐ What is the difference between the mean absolute deviations of Ava's and Mia's shirts?

A   0   C   0.5

B   0.25   D   0.75

Common Core Standard 7.SP.B.3 – Statistics & Probability

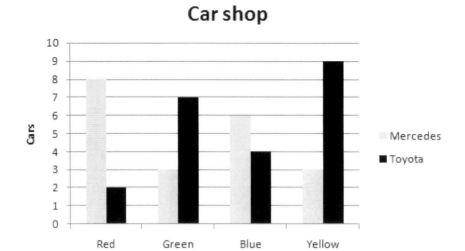

Look at the graph above. How many more Toyota cars does the shop have than Mercedes cars?

A   1   C   3

B   2   D   4

Common Core Standard 7.SP.B.3 – Statistics & Probability

What is the difference between the mean values of Toyota and Mercedes cars?

A   0   C   0.5

B   0. 25   D   0.75

Common Core Standard 7.SP.B.3 – Statistics & Probability

What is the difference between the mean absolute deviations of Toyota and Mercedes cars?

A   0   C   0.5

B   0.25   D   0.75

Name_____

PRACTICE

Common Core Standard 7.SP.B.3 – Statistics & Probability

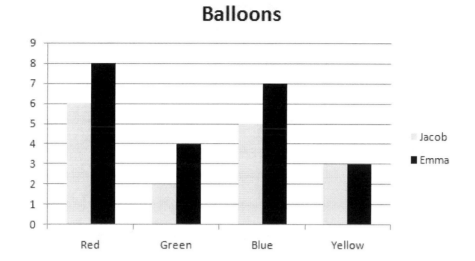

☐ Look at the graph above. How many more balloons does Emma have than Jacob?

A 2   C 6

B 4   D 8

Common Core Standard 7.SP.B.3 – Statistics & Probability

☐ What is the difference between the mean values of Emma's and Jacob's balloons?

A 0   C 1

B 0.5   D 1.5

Common Core Standard 7.SP.B.3 – Statistics & Probability

☐ What is the difference between the mean absolute deviations of Emma's and Jacob's balloons?

A 0   C 0.5

B 0.25   D 0.75

©Teachers' Treasures Publishing

Name_____

PRACTICE

Common Core Standard 7.SP.B.3 – Statistics & Probability

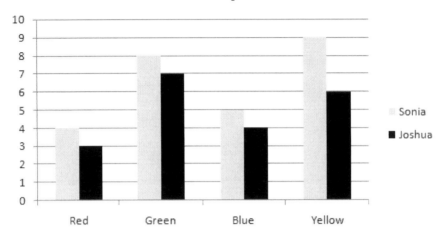

☐ Look at the graph above. How many more birthday hats does Sonia have than Joshua?

A 2 C 6

B 4 D 8

Common Core Standard 7.SP.B.3 – Statistics & Probability

☐ What is the difference between the mean values of Sonia's and Joshua's birthday hats?

A 0 C 1

B 0.5 D 1.5

Common Core Standard 7.SP.B.3 – Statistics & Probability

☐ What is the difference between the mean absolute deviations of Sonia's and Joshua's birthday hats?

A 0 C 0.5

B 0.25 D 0.75

©Teachers' Treasures Publishing

Name

ASSESSMENT

Common Core Standard 7.SP.B.3 – Statistics & Probability

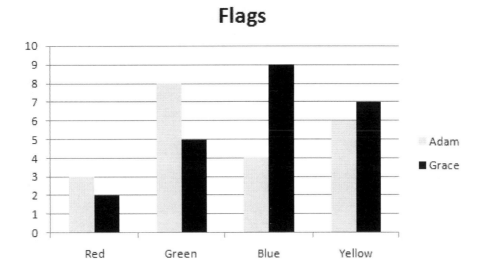

☐ Look at the graph above. How many more flags does Grace have than Adam?

A   1   C   3

B   2   D   4

Common Core Standard 7.SP.B.3 – Statistics & Probability

☐ What is the difference between the mean values of Grace's and Adam's flags?

A   0   C   1

B   0. 5   D   1.5

Common Core Standard 7.SP.B.3 – Statistics & Probability

☐ What is the difference between the mean absolute deviations of Grace's and Adam's flags?

A   0   C   0.5

B   0.25   D   0.75

Name_____

ASSESSMENT

Common Core Standard 7.SP.B.3 – Statistics & Probability

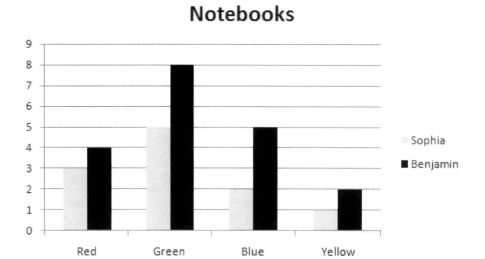

☐ Look at the graph above. How many more notebooks does Benjamin have than Sophia?

A   2   C   6

B   4   D   8

Common Core Standard 7.SP.B.3 – Statistics & Probability

☐ What is the difference between the mean values of Benjamin's and Sophia's notebooks?

A   0   C   2

B   1   D   3

Common Core Standard 7.SP.B.3 – Statistics & Probability

☐ What is the difference between the mean absolute deviations of Benjamin's and Sophia's notebooks?

A   0   C   0.5

B   0.25   D   0.75

Name_____

DIAGNOSTIC

Common Core Standard 7.SP.B.4 – Statistics & Probability

Height of Students in cm				
Boys	186	192	178	180
Girls	164	174	168	170

☐ Look at the table above. Calculate the mean to determine how many centimeters boys are generally taller than girls. Be sure to show your work.

A 4

B 5

C 14

D 15

Common Core Standard 7.SP.B.4 – Statistics & Probability

☐ Calculate the median to determine how many centimeters boys are generally taller than girls. Be sure to show your work.

A 4

B 5

C 14

D 15

Common Core Standard 7.SP.B.4 – Statistics & Probability

☐ Calculate the range to determine the difference of the data for heights of boys and the data for heights of girls. Be sure to show your work.

A 4

B 5

C 14

D 15

©Teachers' Treasures Publishing

Common Core Standard 7.SP.B.4 – Statistics & Probability

Weight of Students in kg					
Boys	83	75	80	69	78
Girls	64	57	63	59	52

☐ Look at the table above. Calculate the mean to determine how many kilograms boys are generally heavier than girls. Be sure to show your work.

A 2

B 11

C 18

D 19

Common Core Standard 7.SP.B.4 – Statistics & Probability

☐ Calculate the median to determine how many kilograms boys are generally heavier than girls. Be sure to show your work.

A 2

B 11

C 18

D 19

Common Core Standard 7.SP.B.4 – Statistics & Probability

☐ Calculate the range to determine how many kilograms the data for boys is greater than the data for girls. Be sure to show your work.

A 2

B 11

C 18

D 19

Name _____

PRACTICE

Common Core Standard 7.SP.B.4 – Statistics & Probability

Height of Players in cm				
Basketball	206	202	196	208
Soccer	168	174	166	172

☐ Look at the table above. Calculate the mean to determine how many centimeters basketball players are generally taller than soccer players. Be sure to show your work.

    A   3

    B   4

    C   33

    D   34

Common Core Standard 7.SP.B.4 – Statistics & Probability

☐ Calculate the median to determine how many centimeters basketball players are generally taller than soccer players. Be sure to show your work.

    A   3

    B   4

    C   33

    D   34

Common Core Standard 7.SP.B.4 – Statistics & Probability

☐ Calculate the range to determine how many centimeters the data for basketball players is greater than the data for soccer players. Be sure to show your work.

    A   3

    B   4

    C   33

    D   34

©Teachers' Treasures Publishing

Name_____

PRACTICE

Common Core Standard 7.SP.B.4 – Statistics & Probability

Weight of Players in kg					
Water polo	109	103	97	102	94
Soccer	65	72	70	69	74

☐ Look at the table above. Calculate the mean to determine how many kilograms water polo players are generally heavier than soccer players. Be sure to show your work.

    A   10

    B   11

    C   31

    D   32

Common Core Standard 7.SP.B.4 – Statistics & Probability

☐ Calculate the median to determine how many kilograms water polo players are generally heavier than soccer players. Be sure to show your work.

    A   10

    B   11

    C   31

    D   32

Common Core Standard 7.SP.B.4 – Statistics & Probability

☐ Calculate the range to determine how many kilograms the data for water polo players is greater in range than the data for soccer players. Be sure to show your work.

    A   6

    B   11

    C   31

    D   32

©Teachers' Treasures Publishing

Common Core Standard 7.SP.B.4 – Statistics & Probability

Age of Employees				
Males	34	26	48	52
Females	36	28	32	40

☐ Look at the table above. Calculate the mean to determine how much older the males are than the females. Be sure to show your work.

    A   6

    B   7

    C   11

    D   14

Common Core Standard 7.SP.B.4 – Statistics & Probability

☐ Calculate the median to determine how much older the males are than the females. Be sure to show your work.

    A   6

    B   7

    C   11

    D   14

Common Core Standard 7.SP.B.4 – Statistics & Probability

☐ Calculate the range to determine the range of data for the males vs. the data for the females. Be sure to show your work.

    A   6

    B   7

    C   11

    D   14

©Teachers' Treasures Publishing

Name_____

PRACTICE

Common Core Standard 7.SP.B.4 – Statistics & Probability

Salary per hour in $					
Males	25	30	15	40	20
Females	35	10	20	15	30

☐ Look at the table above. Calculate the mean to determine how much more are the males paid than females. Be sure to show your work.

A   0

B   2

C   4

D   5

Common Core Standard 7.SP.B.4 – Statistics & Probability

☐ Calculate the median to determine how much more are the males paid than the females. Be sure to show your work.

A   0

B   2

C   4

D   5

Common Core Standard 7.SP.B.4 – Statistics & Probability

☐ Calculate the range to determine how much greater in range is the data for males than for females. Be sure to show your work.

A   0

B   2

C   4

D   5

©Teachers' Treasures Publishing

Name_____

ASSESSMENT

Common Core Standard 7.SP.B.4 – Statistics & Probability

Work Experience				
Males	6	26	12	18
Females	8	34	28	16

☐ Look at the table above. Calculate the mean to determine how much more experienced are the females than the males. Be sure to show your work.

A 6

B 7

C 11

D 14

Common Core Standard 7.SP.B.4 – Statistics & Probability

☐ Calculate the median to determine how much more experienced the females are than males. Be sure to show your work.

A 6

B 7

C 11

D 14

Common Core Standard 7.SP.B.4 – Statistics & Probability

☐ Calculate the range to determine how much greater in range is the data for the females than the data for the males. Be sure to show your work.

A 6

B 7

C 11

D 14

©Teachers' Treasures Publishing

Name_____

ASSESSMENT

Common Core Standard 7.SP.B.4 – Statistics & Probability

Test Scores					
Females	83	33	51	66	77
Males	20	57	64	43	76

☐ Look at the table above. Calculate the mean to determine how much better are the females' score than the males'. Be sure to show your work.

    A   9

    B   10

    C   16

    D   17

Common Core Standard 7.SP.B.4 – Statistics & Probability

☐ Calculate the median to determine how much better is the females' score than the males'. Be sure to show your work.

    A   9

    B   10

    C   16

    D   17

Common Core Standard 7.SP.B.4 – Statistics & Probability

☐ Calculate the range to determine how much greater in range is the data for the males than the data for the females. Be sure to show your work.

    A   9

    B   10

    C   16

    D   6

©Teachers' Treasures Publishing

Name_____

DIAGNOSTIC

Common Core Standard 7.SP.C.5 – Statistics & Probability

☐ There are 7 red cars and 8 blue cars on the parking lot. What type of event is "the randomly selected car is red?" Explain your answer.

- A   likely
- B   unlikely
- C   neither unlikely nor likely
- D   it is not possible to conclude

Common Core Standard 7.SP.C.5 – Statistics & Probability

☐ There are 23 girls and 2 boys in the classroom. What type of event is "the randomly selected student is a boy?" Explain your answer.

- A   likely
- B   unlikely
- C   neither unlikely nor likely
- D   it is not possible to conclude

Common Core Standard 7.SP.C.5 – Statistics & Probability

☐ Cohen has 48 coins and 2 banknotes. What type of event is "a coin is picked?" Explain your answer.

- A   likely
- B   unlikely
- C   neither unlikely nor likely
- D   it is not possible to conclude

©Teachers' Treasures Publishing

Common Core Standard 7.SP.C.5 – Statistics & Probability

☐ There are 350 males and 10 females in the company. What type of event is "the randomly selected employee is a female?" Explain your answer.

A   likely

B   unlikely

C   neither unlikely nor likely

D   it is not possible to conclude

Common Core Standard 7.SP.C.5 – Statistics & Probability

☐ Kamila tosses a coin. What type of event is "the coin landed on heads?" Explain your answer.

A   likely

B   unlikely

C   neither unlikely nor likely

D   it is not possible to conclude

Common Core Standard 7.SP.C.5 – Statistics & Probability

☐ There is an equal number of red and green apples in the basket. What type of event is "the randomly selected apple is green?" Explain your answer.

A   likely

B   unlikely

C   neither unlikely nor likely

D   it is not possible to conclude

Name_____

PRACTICE

Common Core Standard 7.SP.C.5 – Statistics & Probability

☐ For every 10,000 people there is one with an IQ greater than 130. What type of event is "I met a person with an IQ greater than 130 on the street?" Be sure to show your work.

A   likely

B   unlikely

C   neither unlikely nor likely

D   it is not possible to conclude

Common Core Standard 7.SP.C.5 – Statistics & Probability

☐ Jane is rolling a dice. What type of event is "number 2 appeared?" Explain your answer.

A   likely

B   unlikely

C   neither unlikely nor likely

D   it is not possible to conclude

Common Core Standard 7.SP.C.5 – Statistics & Probability

☐ There is an equal number of boys and girls in the school. What type of event is "the randomly selected student is a girl?" Explain your answer.

A   likely

B   unlikely

C   neither unlikely nor likely

D   it is not possible to conclude

©Teachers' Treasures Publishing

Name_____

PRACTICE

Common Core Standard 7.SP.C.5 – Statistics & Probability

☐ There is an equal number of cows and horses on the farm. What type of event is "the randomly selected animal is a cow?" Explain your answer.

- A likely
- B unlikely
- C neither unlikely nor likely
- D it is not possible to conclude

Common Core Standard 7.SP.C.5 – Statistics & Probability

☐ Taila is rolling a dice. What type of event is "an odd number appeared?" Explain your answer.

- A likely
- B unlikely
- C neither unlikely nor likely
- D it is not possible to conclude

Common Core Standard 7.SP.C.5 – Statistics & Probability

☐ 80 of 90 basketball players on the tournament are younger than 30 years old. What type of event is "the randomly selected basketball player is younger than 30 years?" Explain your answer.

- A likely
- B unlikely
- C neither unlikely nor likely
- D it is not possible to conclude

Name_____

PRACTICE

Common Core Standard 7.SP.C.5 – Statistics & Probability

☐ There are 7 red cars and 8 blue cars on the parking lot. What type of event is "the randomly selected car is blue?" Explain your answer.

A   likely

B   unlikely

C   neither unlikely nor likely

D   it is not possible to conclude

Common Core Standard 7.SP.C.5 – Statistics & Probability

☐ There are 23 girls and 2 boys in the classroom. What type of event is "the randomly selected student is a girl?" Explain your answer.

A   likely

B   unlikely

C   neither unlikely nor likely

D   it is not possible to conclude

Common Core Standard 7.SP.C.5 – Statistics & Probability

☐ Phillip has 48 coins and 2 banknotes. What type of event is "a banknote is picked?" Explain your answer.

A   likely

B   unlikely

C   neither unlikely nor likely

D   it is not possible to conclude

©Teachers' Treasures Publishing

Name_____

PRACTICE

Common Core Standard 7.SP.C.5 – Statistics & Probability

☐ There are 350 males and 10 females in the company. What type of event is "the randomly selected employee is a male?" Explain your answer.

A   likely

B   unlikely

C   neither unlikely nor likely

D   it is not possible to conclude

Common Core Standard 7.SP.C.5 – Statistics & Probability

☐ Mia tosses a coin. What type of event is "coin landed on tail"? Be sure to show your work.

A   likely

B   unlikely

C   neither unlikely nor likely

D   it is not possible to conclude

Common Core Standard 7.SP.C.5 – Statistics & Probability

☐ There is an equal number of red and green apples in the basket. What type of event is "randomly selected apple is red"? Be sure to show your work.

A   likely

B   unlikely

C   neither unlikely nor likely

D   it is not possible to conclude

Name_____

ASSESSMENT

Common Core Standard 7.SP.C.5 – Statistics & Probability

☐ **For every 10,000 people there is one with IQ greater than 130. What type of event is "I met a person with IQ less than 130 on the street"? Be sure to show your work.**

A   likely

B   unlikely

C   neither unlikely nor likely

D   it is not possible to conclude

Common Core Standard 7.SP.C.5 – Statistics & Probability

☐ **Mia is rolling a dice. What type of event is "divisor of 12 appeared"? Be sure to show your work.**

A   likely

B   unlikely

C   neither unlikely nor likely

D   it is not possible to conclude

Common Core Standard 7.SP.C.5 – Statistics & Probability

☐ **There is an equal number of boys and girls in the school. What type of event is "randomly selected student is a boy"? Be sure to show your work.**

A   likely

B   unlikely

C   neither unlikely nor likely

D   it is not possible to conclude

©Teachers' Treasures Publishing

Name_____

ASSESSMENT

Common Core Standard 7.SP.C.5 – Statistics & Probability

☐ **There is an equal number of cows and horses on the farm. What type of event is "the animal selected is a horse"? Be sure to show your work.**

A   likely

B   unlikely

C   neither unlikely nor likely

D   it is not possible to conclude

Common Core Standard 7.SP.C.5 – Statistics & Probability

☐ **Mia is rolling a dice. What type of event is "even number appeared"? Be sure to show your work.**

A   likely

B   unlikely

C   neither unlikely nor likely

D   it is not possible to conclude

Common Core Standard 7.SP.C.5 – Statistics & Probability

☐ **80 of 90 basketball players on the tournament are younger than 30 years old. What type of event is "randomly selected basketball player is older than 30 years"? Be sure to show your work.**

A   likely

B   unlikely

C   neither unlikely nor likely

D   it is not possible to conclude

Name_____

DIAGNOSTIC

Common Core Standard 7.SP.C.6 – Statistics & Probability

☐ 3 out of 7 students are girls. How many girls should be estimated among 840 students? Be sure to show your work.

    A   360

    B   400

    C   440

    D   480

Common Core Standard 7.SP.C.6 – Statistics & Probability

☐ A coin is tossed 6 times. How many times is expected that the coin will land on the heads? Be sure to show your work.

    A   3

    B   4

    C   5

    D   6

Common Core Standard 7.SP.C.6 – Statistics & Probability

☐ Marcos picked apples from a bag that contained 32 red and green apples. 3 out of 8 apples were green. What is the best prediction of the number of green apples in the bag? Be sure to show your work.

    A   8

    B   12

    C   16

    D   20

©Teachers' Treasures Publishing

Name_____

DIAGNOSTIC

Common Core Standard 7.SP.C.6 – Statistics & Probability

☐ 2 out of 9 kids on the daycare playground are girls. How many baby-girls should be expected among 495 kids? Be sure to show your work.

- A 100
- B 110
- C 120
- D 130

Common Core Standard 7.SP.C.6 – Statistics & Probability

☐ Two coins are tossed 16 times simultaneously. How many times is expected that both coins will land on the tails? Explain your answer.

- A 3
- B 4
- C 5
- D 6

Common Core Standard 7.SP.C.6 – Statistics & Probability

☐ Cheyenne picked scarves from the box that contained 72 white and black scarves. 2 out of 6 scarves were white. What is the best prediction of the number of white scarves in the box? Be sure to show your work.

- A 24
- B 30
- C 36
- D 48

©Teachers' Treasures Publishing

Name_____

PRACTICE

Common Core Standard 7.SP.C.6 – Statistics & Probability

☐ 4 out of 5 animals in the forest are birds. How many birds should be expected among 135 animals in the forest? Be sure to show your work.

A   100

B   104

C   108

D   112

Common Core Standard 7.SP.C.6 – Statistics & Probability

☐ A dice is rolled 36 times. How many times is expected that the dice will land on number 3? Be sure to show your work.

A   3

B   4

C   5

D   6

Common Core Standard 7.SP.C.6 – Statistics & Probability

☐ Nehemiah picked candies from the jar that contained 91 chocolate and fruit candies. 2 out of 7 candies were chocolate candies. What is the best prediction of the number of chocolate candies in the jar? Be sure to show your work.

A   13

B   26

C   56

D   65

©Teachers' Treasures Publishing

Common Core Standard 7.SP.C.6 – Statistics & Probability

☐ 4 out of 13 tourists in the hotel are international visitors. How many international visitors should be expected among 260 tourists? Be sure to show your work.

A   52

B   80

C   152

D   180

Common Core Standard 7.SP.C.6 – Statistics & Probability

☐ A dice is rolled 18 times. How many times is expected that the dice will land on an even number? Be sure to show your work.

A   3

B   6

C   9

D   12

Common Core Standard 7.SP.C.6 – Statistics & Probability

☐ Marsha picked flowers from the flower shop that had 351 roses and tulips. 6 out of 13 flowers were roses. What is the best prediction of the number of roses at the flower shop? Be sure to show your work.

A   158

B   162

C   189

D   198

Name_____

PRACTICE

Common Core Standard 7.SP.C.6 – Statistics & Probability

☐ **5 out of 8 students live in a house. How many students that live in an apartment should be expected among 960 students? Be sure to show your work.**

- A 360
- B 440
- C 520
- D 600

Common Core Standard 7.SP.C.6 – Statistics & Probability

☐ **Mila tossed 10 flyers in the air. How many flyers are expected to land on the front and how many on the back side? Be sure to show your work.**

- A 3
- B 4
- C 5
- D 6

Common Core Standard 7.SP.C.6 – Statistics & Probability

☐ **Joaquin picked birthday giveaway bags from a basket that contained 45 boy and girl giveaways. 4 out of 9 giveaways were designed for girls. What is the best prediction of the number of boy giveaways in the basket? Be sure to show your work.**

- A 15
- B 20
- C 25
- D 30

©Teachers' Treasures Publishing

Name_____

PRACTICE

Common Core Standard 7.SP.C.6 – Statistics & Probability

☐ **5 out of 12 shoppers at a local mall are men. How many women should be expected among 504 shoppers? Be sure to show your work.**

    A   210

    B   238

    C   266

    D   294

Common Core Standard 7.SP.C.6 – Statistics & Probability

☐ **Two photos are tossed 24 times. How many times is expected that one photo will land face up and the other one face down? Be sure to show your work.**

    A   6

    B   8

    C   10

    D   12

Common Core Standard 7.SP.C.6 – Statistics & Probability

☐ **Karson is picking decorations from a box that contains 63 gold and silver pieces. 7 out of 9 decorations were silver. What is the best prediction of the number of gold decorations in the box? Be sure to show your work.**

    A   14

    B   26

    C   37

    D   49

Name_____

ASSESSMENT

Common Core Standard 7.SP.C.6 – Statistics & Probability

☐ **3 out of 5 animals in the circus are from Africa. How many animals from Africa should be expected among 35 animals in the circus? Be sure to show your work.**

    A   14

    B   15

    C   21

    D   25

Common Core Standard 7.SP.C.6 – Statistics & Probability

☐ **A Monopoly dice is rolled 18 times. How many times is expected that the dice will land on an odd number? Be sure to show your work.**

    A   3

    B   6

    C   9

    D   12

Common Core Standard 7.SP.C.6 – Statistics & Probability

☐ **Arthur is taking out his crystal collection from the storage box that contains 132 pieces of polished and unpolished crystal. 6 out of 11 crystals were polished pieces. What is the best prediction of the number of unpolished crystal pieces in the box? Be sure to show your work.**

    A   48

    B   60

    C   72

    D   84

©Teachers' Treasures Publishing

Name_____

ASSESSMENT

Common Core Standard 7.SP.C.6 – Statistics & Probability

☐ 5 out of 7 drivers in the school zone are teenagers. How many teenagers should be expected among 224 drivers in the school zone? Be sure to show your work.

    A   64

    B   96

    C   128

    D   160

Common Core Standard 7.SP.C.6 – Statistics & Probability

☐ A dice is rolled 12 times. How many times is expected that the dice will land on a number which is divisor of 12? Be sure to show your work.

    A   8

    B   9

    C   10

    D   11

Common Core Standard 7.SP.C.6 – Statistics & Probability

☐ Lena is picking up desserts for a large reception. The bakery has 368 cupcakes and cookies. 7 out of 16 pieces of dessert were cupcakes. What is the best prediction of the number of cookies at the bakery shop? Be sure to show your work.

    A   161

    B   183

    C   207

    D   225

©Teachers' Treasures Publishing

Name_____

DIAGNOSTIC

Common Core Standard 7.SP.C.7.A – Statistics & Probability

☐ There are 18 girls and 6 boys competing at the school music performance. In order to perform the first, what is the probability that a randomly selected student will be a girl? Be sure to show your work.

A $\dfrac{1}{4}$

B $\dfrac{1}{3}$

C $\dfrac{2}{3}$

D $\dfrac{3}{4}$

Common Core Standard 7.SP.C.7.A – Statistics & Probability

☐ What is the probability of picking a red marble from the box of 8 red, 12 green, and 20 blue marbles? Be sure to show your work.

A 0.2

B 0.3

C 0.5

D 0.8

Common Core Standard 7.SP.C.7.A – Statistics & Probability

☐ Rafael selects a card from the deck of 52 cards. What is the probability that he will select a red queen? Be sure to show your work.

A $\dfrac{1}{26}$

B $\dfrac{1}{13}$

C 0.25

D 50%

©Teachers' Treasures Publishing

Name _____

DIAGNOSTIC

Common Core Standard 7.SP.C.7.A – Statistics & Probability

☐ There are 18 white and 12 red ribbons in Ashley's ribbon drawer. What is the probability that a randomly selected ribbon will be white? Be sure to show your work.

- A 30%
- B 40%
- C 50%
- D 60%

Common Core Standard 7.SP.C.7.A – Statistics & Probability

☐ What is the probability of picking a tulip from the bouquet of 15 roses, 20 tulips, and 25 violets? Be sure to show your work.

- A 0.2
- B 0.33
- C 0.4
- D 0.67

Common Core Standard 7.SP.C.7.A – Statistics & Probability

☐ Rowan selects a card from the deck of 52 cards. What is the probability that he will select a diamond? Be sure to show your work.

- A $\frac{1}{26}$
- B $\frac{1}{13}$
- C $\frac{1}{4}$
- D $\frac{1}{2}$

©Teachers' Treasures Publishing

Name_____

PRACTICE

Common Core Standard 7.SP.C.7.A – Statistics & Probability

☐ There are 30 goats and 20 pigs on the farm. What is the probability that a randomly selected animal will be a goat? Be sure to show your work.

A $\frac{3}{5}$

B $\frac{2}{3}$

C $\frac{1}{2}$

D $\frac{2}{5}$

Common Core Standard 7.SP.C.7.A – Statistics & Probability

☐ What is the probability of picking a red piece of paper from the stack of 6 red, 4 green, and 10 yellow pieces of paper? Be sure to show your work.

A 0.2

B 0.3

C 0.5

D 0.6

Common Core Standard 7.SP.C.7.A – Statistics & Probability

☐ Felix selects a card from the deck of 52 cards. What is the probability that he will select a black card? Be sure to show your work.

A $\frac{1}{26}$

B $\frac{1}{13}$

C 0.25

D 50%

Name_____

PRACTICE

Common Core Standard 7.SP.C.7.A – Statistics & Probability

☐ **There are 15 children and 35 adults on the bus. What is the probability that a randomly selected passenger will be a child? Be sure to show your work.**

A   15%

B   30%

C   35%

D   70%

Common Core Standard 7.SP.C.7.A – Statistics & Probability

☐ **What is the probability of picking a cherry from the bag of 12 cherries, 4 walnuts, and 8 plums? Be sure to show your work.**

A   0.12

B   0.25

C   0.33

D   0.5

Common Core Standard 7.SP.C.7.A – Statistics & Probability

☐ **Rowan selects a card from the deck of 52 cards. What is the probability that he will select a jack? Be sure to show your work.**

A $\frac{1}{26}$

B $\frac{1}{13}$

C $\frac{1}{4}$

D $\frac{1}{2}$

©Teachers' Treasures Publishing

Name_____

PRACTICE

Common Core Standard 7.SP.C.7.A – Statistics & Probability

☐ There are 16 girls and 8 boys in the choir. What is the probability that a randomly selected singer will be a boy? Be sure to show your work.

A $\dfrac{1}{4}$

B $\dfrac{1}{3}$

C $\dfrac{2}{3}$

D $\dfrac{3}{4}$

Common Core Standard 7.SP.C.7.A – Statistics & Probability

☐ What is the probability of picking a red or a blue baloon from the bunch of 8 red, 12 white, and 20 blue baloons? Be sure to show your work.

A 0.2

B 0.3

C 0.5

D 0.7

Common Core Standard 7.SP.C.7.A – Statistics & Probability

☐ Emilio selects a card from the deck of 52 cards. What is the probability that he will select an ace? Be sure to show your work.

A $\dfrac{1}{26}$

B $\dfrac{1}{13}$

C 0.25

D 50%

©Teachers' Treasures Publishing

Name_____

PRACTICE

Common Core Standard 7.SP.C.7.A – Statistics & Probability

☐ There are 54 black and 36 red pencils in the pencil box. What is the probability that a randomly selected pencil will be red? Be sure to show your work.

A   30%

B   40%

C   50%

D   60%

Common Core Standard 7.SP.C.7.A – Statistics & Probability

☐ What is the probability of picking a rose or a violet from the bucket full of 15 roses, 20 tulips, and 25 violets? Be sure to show your work.

A   0.2

B   0.33

C   0.4

D   0.67

Common Core Standard 7.SP.C.7.A – Statistics & Probability

☐ Maverick selects a card from the deck of 52 cards. What is the probability that he will select a heart? Be sure to show your work.

A $\dfrac{1}{26}$

B $\dfrac{1}{13}$

C $\dfrac{1}{4}$

D $\dfrac{1}{2}$

Name_____

ASSESSMENT

Common Core Standard 7.SP.C.7.A – Statistics & Probability

☐ There are 27 pictures of blond kids and 18 pictures of brunette kids in the kids' model selection album. What is the probability that a randomly selected picture will be a one of a brunette kid? Be sure to show your work.

A $\frac{3}{5}$

B $\frac{2}{3}$

C $\frac{1}{2}$

D $\frac{2}{5}$

Common Core Standard 7.SP.C.7.A – Statistics & Probability

☐ What is the probability of picking a red or a green cookie from the bag of 6 red, 4 green, and 10 yellow cookies? Be sure to show your work.

A   0.2

B   0.3

C   0.5

D   0.6

Common Core Standard 7.SP.C.7.A – Statistics & Probability

☐ Tyson selects a card from the deck of 52 cards. What is the probability that he will select a red card? Be sure to show your work.

A $\frac{1}{26}$

B $\frac{1}{13}$

C   0.25

D   50%

Name_____

ASSESSMENT

Common Core Standard 7.SP.C.7.A – Statistics & Probability

☐ There are 32 male and 8 female athletes all completing a 10K run. What is the probability that a randomly selected athlete for a TV interview will be a female? Be sure to show your work.

A 15%

B 20%

C 35%

D 80%

Common Core Standard 7.SP.C.7.A – Statistics & Probability

☐ What is the probability of picking a blueberry or a rasberry from a plate fill of 12 blackberries, 4 blueberries and 8 rasberries? Be sure to show your work.

A 0.12

B 0.25

C 0.33

D 0.5

Common Core Standard 7.SP.C.7.A – Statistics & Probability

☐ Raymond selects a card from the deck of 52 cards. What is the probability that he will select a black ace? Be sure to show your work.

A $\dfrac{1}{26}$

B $\dfrac{1}{13}$

C $\dfrac{1}{4}$

D $\dfrac{1}{2}$

Name_____

DIAGNOSTIC

Common Core Standard 7.SP.C.7.B – Statistics & Probability

Red fruit	2	5	2	4
Green fruit	6	12	7	11
Yellow fruit	4	7	4	8

☐ The table above shows the number of fruits in different baskets. What is the approximate probability that a randomly selected fruit will be red? Be sure to show your work.

A $\dfrac{1}{2}$ C $\dfrac{1}{4}$

B $\dfrac{1}{3}$ D $\dfrac{1}{6}$

Common Core Standard 7.SP.C.7.B – Statistics & Probability

☐ What is the approximate probability that a randomly selected fruit will be green? Be sure to show your work.

A $\dfrac{1}{2}$ C $\dfrac{1}{4}$

B $\dfrac{1}{3}$ D $\dfrac{1}{6}$

Common Core Standard 7.SP.C.7.B – Statistics & Probability

☐ What is the approximate probability that a randomly selected fruit will be yellow? Be sure to show your work.

A $\dfrac{1}{2}$ C $\dfrac{1}{4}$

B $\dfrac{1}{3}$ D $\dfrac{1}{6}$

©Teachers' Treasures Publishing

Name_____

DIAGNOSTIC

Common Core Standard 7.SP.C.7.B – Statistics & Probability

Honda	2	8	6	4
BMW	5	19	15	11
Mercedes	3	13	10	6

☐ The table above shows the number of cars on different parking lots. What is the approximate probability that a randomly selected car will be Honda? Be sure to show your work.

A $\dfrac{1}{2}$ C $\dfrac{1}{5}$

B $\dfrac{3}{10}$ D $\dfrac{1}{6}$

Common Core Standard 7.SP.C.7.B – Statistics & Probability

☐ What is the approximate probability that a randomly selected car will be BMW? Be sure to show your work.

A $\dfrac{1}{2}$ C $\dfrac{1}{5}$

B $\dfrac{3}{10}$ D $\dfrac{1}{6}$

Common Core Standard 7.SP.C.7.B – Statistics & Probability

☐ What is the approximate probability that a randomly selected car will be Mercedes? Be sure to show your work.

A $\dfrac{1}{2}$ C $\dfrac{1}{5}$

B $\dfrac{3}{10}$ D $\dfrac{1}{6}$

©Teachers' Treasures Publishing

Common Core Standard 7.SP.C.7.B – Statistics & Probability

Red balloons	4	17	12	20
Green balloons	2	8	7	10
Blue balloons	10	40	29	49

☐ The table above shows the number of balloons in different bunches. What is the approximate probability that a randomly selected balloon will be red? Be sure to show your work.

A $\dfrac{1}{8}$ C $\dfrac{1}{2}$

B $\dfrac{1}{4}$ D $\dfrac{5}{8}$

Common Core Standard 7.SP.C.7.B – Statistics & Probability

☐ What is the approximate probability that a randomly selected balloon will be green? Be sure to show your work.

A $\dfrac{1}{8}$ C $\dfrac{1}{2}$

B $\dfrac{1}{4}$ D $\dfrac{5}{8}$

Common Core Standard 7.SP.C.7.B – Statistics & Probability

☐ What is the approximate probability that a randomly selected balloon will be blue? Be sure to show your work.

A $\dfrac{1}{8}$ C $\dfrac{1}{2}$

B $\dfrac{1}{4}$ D $\dfrac{5}{8}$

Name_____

PRACTICE

Common Core Standard 7.SP.C.7.B – Statistics & Probability

Roses	30	21	10	49
Tulips	20	14	7	36
Violets	12	8	4	20

☐ The table above shows the number of flowers in different bouquets. What is the approximate probability that a randomly selected flower will be rose? Be sure to show your work.

A $\dfrac{1}{2}$ C $\dfrac{1}{4}$

B $\dfrac{1}{3}$ D $\dfrac{1}{5}$

Common Core Standard 7.SP.C.7.B – Statistics & Probability

☐ What is the approximate probability that a randomly selected flower will be tulip? Be sure to show your work.

A $\dfrac{1}{2}$ C $\dfrac{1}{4}$

B $\dfrac{1}{3}$ D $\dfrac{1}{5}$

Common Core Standard 7.SP.C.7.B – Statistics & Probability

☐ What is the approximate probability that a randomly selected flower will be violet? Be sure to show your work.

A $\dfrac{1}{2}$ C $\dfrac{1}{4}$

B $\dfrac{1}{3}$ D $\dfrac{1}{5}$

©Teachers' Treasures Publishing

Name_____

PRACTICE

Common Core Standard 7.SP.C.7.B – Statistics & Probability

40 Watts bulbs	61	10	39	30
60 Watts bulbs	90	15	61	46
100 Watts bulbs	29	5	20	14

☐ The table above shows the number of bulbs in different packs. What is the approximate probability that a randomly selected bulb will be 40 Watts? Be sure to show your work.

A $\dfrac{1}{2}$ C $\dfrac{1}{4}$

B $\dfrac{1}{3}$ D $\dfrac{1}{6}$

Common Core Standard 7.SP.C.7.B – Statistics & Probability

☐ What is the approximate probability that a randomly selected bulb will be 60 Watts? Be sure to show your work.

A $\dfrac{1}{2}$ C $\dfrac{1}{4}$

B $\dfrac{1}{3}$ D $\dfrac{1}{6}$

Common Core Standard 7.SP.C.7.B – Statistics & Probability

☐ What is the approximate probability that a randomly selected bulb will be 100 Watts? Be sure to show your work.

A $\dfrac{1}{2}$ C $\dfrac{1}{4}$

B $\dfrac{1}{3}$ D $\dfrac{1}{6}$

©Teachers' Treasures Publishing

Name_____

PRACTICE

Common Core Standard 7.SP.C.7.B – Statistics & Probability

Apricot	14	3	13	9
Pear	5	1	4	3
Orange	11	2	9	6

☐ The table above shows the number of fruits in different boxes. What is the approximate probability that a randomly selected fruit will be apricot? Be sure to show your work.

A $\dfrac{1}{2}$ C $\dfrac{1}{4}$

B $\dfrac{1}{3}$ D $\dfrac{1}{6}$

Common Core Standard 7.SP.C.7.B – Statistics & Probability

☐ What is the approximate probability that a randomly selected fruit will be pear? Be sure to show your work.

A $\dfrac{1}{2}$ C $\dfrac{1}{4}$

B $\dfrac{1}{3}$ D $\dfrac{1}{6}$

Common Core Standard 7.SP.C.7.B – Statistics & Probability

☐ What is the approximate probability that a randomly selected fruit will be orange? Be sure to show your work.

A $\dfrac{1}{2}$ C $\dfrac{1}{4}$

B $\dfrac{1}{3}$ D $\dfrac{1}{6}$

©Teachers' Treasures Publishing

Name_____

ASSESSMENT

Common Core Standard 7.SP.C.7.B – Statistics & Probability

Onion	16	11	4	19
Potato	4	3	1	5
Tomato	59	46	15	76

☐ The table above shows the number of vegetables in different boxes. What is the approximate probability that a randomly selected vegetable will be onion? Be sure to show your work.

A $\dfrac{1}{20}$ C $\dfrac{3}{4}$

B $\dfrac{1}{5}$ D $\dfrac{7}{8}$

Common Core Standard 7.SP.C.7.B – Statistics & Probability

☐ What is the approximate probability that a randomly selected vegetable will be potato? Be sure to show your work.

A $\dfrac{1}{20}$ C $\dfrac{3}{4}$

B $\dfrac{1}{5}$ D $\dfrac{7}{8}$

Common Core Standard 7.SP.C.7.B – Statistics & Probability

☐ What is the approximate probability that a randomly selected vegetable will be tomato? Be sure to show your work.

A $\dfrac{1}{20}$ C $\dfrac{3}{4}$

B $\dfrac{1}{5}$ D $\dfrac{7}{8}$

©Teachers' Treasures Publishing

Name_____

ASSESSMENT

Common Core Standard 7.SP.C.7.B – Statistics & Probability

White socks	25	32	8	41
Blue socks	12	15	4	19
Black socks	35	49	12	60

☐ The table above shows the number of socks in different boxes. What is the approximate probability that a randomly selected pair of socks will be white? Be sure to show your work.

A $\frac{1}{6}$ C $\frac{1}{3}$

B $\frac{1}{4}$ D $\frac{1}{2}$

Common Core Standard 7.SP.C.7.B – Statistics & Probability

☐ What is the approximate probability that a randomly selected pair of socks will be blue? Be sure to show your work.

A $\frac{1}{6}$ C $\frac{1}{3}$

B $\frac{1}{4}$ D $\frac{1}{2}$

Common Core Standard 7.SP.C.7.B – Statistics & Probability

☐ What is the approximate probability that a randomly selected pair of socks will be black? Be sure to show your work.

A $\frac{1}{6}$ C $\frac{1}{3}$

B $\frac{1}{4}$ D $\frac{1}{2}$

Name_____

DIAGNOSTIC

Common Core Standard 7.SP.C.8.A – Statistics & Probability

"There are 8 green and 6 blue marbles in a bag. Pick a marble and put it back in the bag. Pick one more marble."

☐ What is the probability that both selected marbles are green? Be sure to show your work.

- A $\dfrac{1}{7}$
- B $\dfrac{9}{49}$
- C $\dfrac{16}{49}$
- D $\dfrac{12}{49}$

Common Core Standard 7.SP.C.8.A – Statistics & Probability

☐ What is the probability that the first selected marble is green, and the second selected marble is blue? Be sure to show your work.

- A $\dfrac{1}{7}$
- B $\dfrac{9}{49}$
- C $\dfrac{16}{49}$
- D $\dfrac{12}{49}$

Common Core Standard 7.SP.C.8.A – Statistics & Probability

☐ What is the probability that both selected marbles are blue? Be sure to show your work.

- A $\dfrac{1}{7}$
- B $\dfrac{9}{49}$
- C $\dfrac{16}{49}$
- D $\dfrac{12}{49}$

©Teachers' Treasures Publishing

Name_____

DIAGNOSTIC

Common Core Standard 7.SP.C.8.A – Statistics & Probability

"There are 8 green and 6 blue cookies in a bag. Pick a cookie and eat it. Pick one more cookie."

☐ What is the probability that both selected cookies are green? Be sure to show your work.

A $\dfrac{4}{13}$ C $\dfrac{24}{91}$

B $\dfrac{15}{91}$ D $\dfrac{3}{13}$

Common Core Standard 7.SP.C.8.A – Statistics & Probability

☐ What is the probability that the first selected cookie is green, and the second selected cookie is blue? Be sure to show your work.

A $\dfrac{4}{13}$ C $\dfrac{24}{91}$

B $\dfrac{15}{91}$ D $\dfrac{3}{13}$

Common Core Standard 7.SP.C.8.A – Statistics & Probability

☐ What is the probability that both selected cookies are blue? Be sure to show your work.

A $\dfrac{4}{13}$ C $\dfrac{24}{91}$

B $\dfrac{15}{91}$ D $\dfrac{3}{13}$

©Teachers' Treasures Publishing

Name_____

PRACTICE

Common Core Standard 7.SP.C.8.A – Statistics & Probability

"There are 4 red and 8 green apples in a bag. Pick an apple and put it back in the bag. Pick one more apple."

☐ What is the probability that both selected apples are red? Be sure to show your work.

    A $\dfrac{1}{9}$ C $\dfrac{1}{3}$

    B $\dfrac{2}{9}$ D $\dfrac{4}{9}$

Common Core Standard 7.SP.C.8.A – Statistics & Probability

☐ What is the probability that the first selected apple is green, and the second one is red? Be sure to show your work.

    A $\dfrac{1}{9}$ C $\dfrac{1}{3}$

    B $\dfrac{2}{9}$ D $\dfrac{4}{9}$

Common Core Standard 7.SP.C.8.A – Statistics & Probability

☐ What is the probability that both selected apples are green? Be sure to show your work.

    A $\dfrac{1}{9}$ C $\dfrac{1}{3}$

    B $\dfrac{2}{9}$ D $\dfrac{4}{9}$

©Teachers' Treasures Publishing

Common Core Standard 7.SP.C.8.A – Statistics & Probability

"There are 4 red and 8 green plums in a bag. Pick a plum and eat it. Pick one more plum."

☐ What is the probability that both selected plums are red? Be sure to show your work.

A $\dfrac{2}{11}$

B $\dfrac{8}{33}$

C $\dfrac{1}{11}$

D $\dfrac{14}{33}$

Common Core Standard 7.SP.C.8.A – Statistics & Probability

☐ What is the probability that the first selected plum is green, and the second selected plum is red? Be sure to show your work.

A $\dfrac{2}{11}$

B $\dfrac{8}{33}$

C $\dfrac{1}{11}$

D $\dfrac{14}{33}$

Common Core Standard 7.SP.C.8.A – Statistics & Probability

☐ What is the probability that both selected plums are green? Be sure to show your work.

A $\dfrac{2}{11}$

B $\dfrac{8}{33}$

C $\dfrac{1}{11}$

D $\dfrac{14}{33}$

©Teachers' Treasures Publishing

Name_____

PRACTICE

Common Core Standard 7.SP.C.8.A – Statistics & Probability

"There are 8 carnations and 2 tulips in a bouquet. Pick a flower and put it back. Pick one more flower."

☐ What is the probability that both selected flowers are carnations? Be sure to show your work.

A $\dfrac{1}{25}$ C $\dfrac{9}{25}$

B $\dfrac{4}{25}$ D $\dfrac{16}{25}$

Common Core Standard 7.SP.C.8.A – Statistics & Probability

☐ What is the probability that the first selected flower is carnation, while the second selected flower is tulip? Be sure to show your work.

A $\dfrac{1}{25}$ C $\dfrac{9}{25}$

B $\dfrac{4}{25}$ D $\dfrac{16}{25}$

Common Core Standard 7.SP.C.8.A – Statistics & Probability

☐ What is the probability that both selected flowers are tulips? Be sure to show your work.

A $\dfrac{1}{25}$ C $\dfrac{9}{25}$

B $\dfrac{4}{25}$ D $\dfrac{16}{25}$

PRACTICE

Name_____

Common Core Standard 7.SP.C.8.A – Statistics & Probability

"There are 8 carnations and 2 tulips in a bouquet. Pick a flower and give it to your friend. Pick one more flower."

☐ What is the probability that both selected flowers are carnations? Be sure to show your work.

- A $\dfrac{1}{45}$
- B $\dfrac{8}{45}$
- C $\dfrac{18}{45}$
- D $\dfrac{28}{45}$

Common Core Standard 7.SP.C.8.A – Statistics & Probability

☐ What is the probability that the first selected flower is carnation, while the second one flower is tulip? Be sure to show your work.

- A $\dfrac{1}{45}$
- B $\dfrac{8}{45}$
- C $\dfrac{18}{45}$
- D $\dfrac{28}{45}$

Common Core Standard 7.SP.C.8.A – Statistics & Probability

☐ What is the probability that both selected flowers are tulips? Be sure to show your work.

- A $\dfrac{1}{45}$
- B $\dfrac{8}{45}$
- C $\dfrac{18}{45}$
- D $\dfrac{28}{45}$

©Teachers' Treasures Publishing

Name_____

ASSESSMENT

Common Core Standard 7.SP.C.8.A – Statistics & Probability

"There are 90 paperclips and 60 pins in a box. Pick an item and put it back. Pick one more item."

☐ What is the probability that both selected items are paperclips? Be sure to show your work.

A $\dfrac{1}{25}$ C $\dfrac{6}{25}$

B $\dfrac{4}{25}$ D $\dfrac{9}{25}$

Common Core Standard 7.SP.C.8.A – Statistics & Probability

☐ What is the probability that the first selected item is pin, while the second selected item is paperclip? Be sure to show your work.

A $\dfrac{1}{25}$ C $\dfrac{6}{25}$

B $\dfrac{4}{25}$ D $\dfrac{9}{25}$

Common Core Standard 7.SP.C.8.A – Statistics & Probability

☐ What is the probability that both selected items are pins? Be sure to show your work.

A $\dfrac{1}{25}$ C $\dfrac{6}{25}$

B $\dfrac{4}{25}$ D $\dfrac{9}{25}$

Name_____

ASSESSMENT

Common Core Standard 7.SP.C.8.A – Statistics & Probability

"There are 90 paperclips and 60 pins in the box. Pick an item and use it for your project. Pick one more item."

☐ What is the probability that both selected items are paperclips? Be sure to show your work.

A $\dfrac{118}{745}$ C $\dfrac{6}{149}$

B $\dfrac{267}{745}$ D $\dfrac{36}{149}$

Common Core Standard 7.SP.C.8.A – Statistics & Probability

☐ What is the probability that the first selected item is pin, and the second item is paperclip? Be sure to show your work.

A $\dfrac{118}{745}$ C $\dfrac{6}{149}$

B $\dfrac{267}{745}$ D $\dfrac{36}{149}$

Common Core Standard 7.SP.C.8.A – Statistics & Probability

☐ What is the probability that both selected items are pins? Be sure to show your work.

A $\dfrac{118}{745}$ C $\dfrac{6}{149}$

B $\dfrac{267}{745}$ D $\dfrac{36}{149}$

©Teachers' Treasures Publishing

Name_____

DIAGNOSTIC

Common Core Standard 7.SP.C.8.B – Statistics & Probability

☐ Vivienne is rolling 2 dice. What is the number of all possible outcomes? Be sure to show your work.

    A   6

    B   12

    C   18

    D   36

Common Core Standard 7.SP.C.8.B – Statistics & Probability

☐ Diana flips 2 coins. What is the number of all possible outcomes? Be sure to show your work.

    A   2

    B   4

    C   6

    D   8

Common Core Standard 7.SP.C.8.B – Statistics & Probability

☐ There are 5 boys and 6 girls. How many teams of two with 1 boy and 1 girl can be formed? Be sure to show your work.

    A   5

    B   6

    C   11

    D   30

Name_____

DIAGNOSTIC

Common Core Standard 7.SP.C.8.B – Statistics & Probability

☐ Trenton roles 3 dice. What is the number of all possible outcomes? Be sure to show your work.

A   6
B   18
C   216
D   666

Common Core Standard 7.SP.C.8.B – Statistics & Probability

☐ Eduardo flips 3 coins. What is the number of all possible outcomes? Be sure to show your work.

A   2
B   4
C   6
D   8

Common Core Standard 7.SP.C.8.B – Statistics & Probability

☐ Melody has 4 dogs and 7 cats. How many pairs of a dog and a cat can be formed? Be sure to show your work.

A   11
B   28
C   47
D   74

©Teachers' Treasures Publishing

Name_____

PRACTICE

Common Core Standard 7.SP.C.8.B – Statistics & Probability

☐ **Lauren roles a dice and picks a card. What is the number of all possible outcomes? Be sure to show your work.**

A   11

B   30

C   56

D   65

Common Core Standard 7.SP.C.8.B – Statistics & Probability

☐ **Adalynn flips a coin and rolls a dice. What is the number of all possible outcomes? Be sure to show your work.**

A   2

B   6

C   8

D   12

Common Core Standard 7.SP.C.8.B – Statistics & Probability

☐ **Ezra has 5 shirts and 3 hats. How many different combinations of a shirt and a hat can he wear? Be sure to show your work.**

A   15

B   30

C   35

D   53

©Teachers' Treasures Publishing

Name_____

PRACTICE

Common Core Standard 7.SP.C.8.B – Statistics & Probability

☐ **Tristan flips a coin and picks a card. What is the number of all possible outcomes? Be sure to show your work.**

A   7

B   10

C   25

D   52

Common Core Standard 7.SP.C.8.B – Statistics & Probability

☐ **Carlos flips a coin, rolls a dice, and picks a card. What is the number of all possible outcomes? Be sure to show your work.**

A   10

B   12

C   30

D   60

Common Core Standard 7.SP.C.8.B – Statistics & Probability

☐ **Chloe has 4 pairs of shoes and 9 pairs of socks. How many different combinations of a pair of shoes and a pair of socks can she wear? Be sure to show your work.**

A   36

B   40

C   49

D   50

©Teachers' Treasures Publishing

Name _____

PRACTICE

Common Core Standard 7.SP.C.8.B – Statistics & Probability

☐   **Micah flips 2 coins and picks a card. What is the number of all possible outcomes? Be sure to show your work.**

A   2

B   5

C   10

D   20

Common Core Standard 7.SP.C.8.B – Statistics & Probability

☐   **Carter rolls 2 dice and picks a card. What is the number of all possible outcomes? Be sure to show your work.**

A   17

B   30

C   36

D   180

Common Core Standard 7.SP.C.8.B – Statistics & Probability

☐   **Eleanor has 7 jackets and 2 skirts. How many different combinations of a jacket and a skirt can she wear? Be sure to show your work.**

A   9

B   14

C   27

D   72

©Teachers' Treasures Publishing

Name_____

PRACTICE

Common Core Standard 7.SP.C.8.B – Statistics & Probability

☐ **Megan flips 2 coins and rolls a dice. What is the number of all possible outcomes? Be sure to show your work.**

A   2

B   3

C   6

D   24

Common Core Standard 7.SP.C.8.B – Statistics & Probability

☐ **Jasmin rolls 2 dice and flips a coin. What is the number of all possible outcomes? Be sure to show your work.**

A   9

B   18

C   36

D   72

Common Core Standard 7.SP.C.8.B – Statistics & Probability

☐ **Gautham has 8 notebooks and 4 pencils. How many different combinations of a notebook and a pencil can he make? Be sure to show your work.**

A   4

B   8

C   12

D   32

©Teachers' Treasures Publishing

Name_____

ASSESSMENT

Common Core Standard 7.SP.C.8.B – Statistics & Probability

☐ Thomas flips a coin and picks a card from the deck of 52 cards. What is the number of all possible outcomes? Be sure to show your work.

    A   2

    B   52

    C   54

    D   104

Common Core Standard 7.SP.C.8.B – Statistics & Probability

☐ Miles rolls a dice and picks a card from the deck of 32 cards. What is the number of all possible outcomes? Be sure to show your work.

    A   6

    B   32

    C   38

    D   192

Common Core Standard 7.SP.C.8.B – Statistics & Probability

☐ Rachel has 3 umbrellas and 4 rain jackets. How many different combinations of an umbrella and a rain jacket can she make? Be sure to show your work.

    A   7

    B   12

    C   34

    D   43

©Teachers' Treasures Publishing

Name_____

ASSESSMENT

Common Core Standard 7.SP.C.8.B – Statistics & Probability

☐ Pedro flips a coin and spins a spinner. What is the number of all possible outcomes? Be sure to show your work.

A 8

B 12

C 16

D 32

Common Core Standard 7.SP.C.8.B – Statistics & Probability

☐ Isaac rolls a dice and spins a spinner. What is the number of all possible outcomes? Be sure to show your work.

A 6

B 48

C 68

D 86

Common Core Standard 7.SP.C.8.B – Statistics & Probability

☐ Vera rolls a dice, flips a coin, spins a spinner, and picks a card. What is the number of all possible outcomes? Be sure to show your work.

A 48

B 96

C 192

D 384

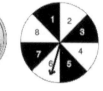

©Teachers' Treasures Publishing

Name_____

DIAGNOSTIC

Common Core Standard 7.SP.C.8.C – Statistics & Probability

"30% of students are girls"

☐ What is the probability that it will take at least 3 students to find one girl? Be sure to show your work.

    A   6.3%

    B   6.7%

    C   14.7%

    D   21%

Common Core Standard 7.SP.C.8.C – Statistics & Probability

☐ What is the probability that it will take at least 3 students to find one boy? Be sure to show your work.

    A   6.3%

    B   6.7%

    C   14.7%

    D   21%

Common Core Standard 7.SP.C.8.C – Statistics & Probability

☐ What is the probability that it will take at least 2 students to find one girl? Be sure to show your work.

    A   21%

    B   30%

    C   50%

    D   70%

©Teachers' Treasures Publishing

Common Core Standard 7.SP.C.8.C – Statistics & Probability

"60% of students weigh more than 120 pounds"

☐ What is the probability that it will take at least 2 students to find one who weighs more than 120 pounds? Be sure to show your work.

- A 12%
- B 24%
- C 50%
- D 60%

Common Core Standard 7.SP.C.8.C – Statistics & Probability

☐ What is the probability that it will take at least 3 students to find one who weighs more than 120 pounds? Be sure to show your work.

- A 9.4%
- B 9.6%
- C 14.4%
- D 14.6%

Common Core Standard 7.SP.C.8.C – Statistics & Probability

☐ What is the probability that it will take at least 3 students to find one who weighs 120 pounds or less? Be sure to show your work.

- A 9.4%
- B 9.6%
- C 14.4%
- D 14.6%

Name_____

PRACTICE

Common Core Standard 7.SP.C.8.C – Statistics & Probability

"20% of animals on the farm are goats"

☐ What is the probability that it will take at least 2 animals to find one goat? Be sure to show your work.

    A   10.24%

    B   12.8%

    C   16%

    D   50%

Common Core Standard 7.SP.C.8.C – Statistics & Probability

☐ What is the probability that it will take at least 3 animals to find one goat? Be sure to show your work.

    A   10.24%

    B   12.8%

    C   16%

    D   20%

Common Core Standard 7.SP.C.8.C – Statistics & Probability

☐ What is the probability that it will take at least 4 animals to find one goat? Be sure to show your work.

    A   10.24%

    B   12.8%

    C   16%

    D   20%

©Teachers' Treasures Publishing

Common Core Standard 7.SP.C.8.C – Statistics & Probability

"15% of drivers have less than 2 years of experience"

☐ What is the probability that it will take at least 2 drivers to find one with less than 2 years of experience in driving? Be sure to show your work.

- A   1.91%
- B   10.84%
- C   12.75%
- D   50%

Common Core Standard 7.SP.C.8.C – Statistics & Probability

☐ What is the probability that it will take at least 3 drivers to find one with 2 or more years of experience in driving? Be sure to show your work.

- A   1.91%
- B   10.84%
- C   12.75%
- D   15%

Common Core Standard 7.SP.C.8.C – Statistics & Probability

☐ What is the probability that it will take at least 3 drivers to find one with less than 2 years of experience in driving? Be sure to show your work.

- A   1.91%
- B   10.84%
- C   12.75%
- D   15%

Common Core Standard 7.SP.C.8.C – Statistics & Probability

"25% of employees are males"

☐ What is the probability that it will take at least 2 employees to find one female? Be sure to show your work.

    A   1.17%

    B   14.06%

    C   18.75%

    D   50%

Common Core Standard 7.SP.C.8.C – Statistics & Probability

☐ What is the probability that it will take at least 4 employees to find one female? Be sure to show your work.

    A   1.17%

    B   14.06%

    C   18.75%

    D   25%

Common Core Standard 7.SP.C.8.C – Statistics & Probability

☐ What is the probability that it will take at least 3 employees to find one male? Be sure to show your work.

    A   1.17%

    B   14.06%

    C   18.75%

    D   25%

Common Core Standard 7.SP.C.8.C – Statistics & Probability

"70% of senior students have driving license"

☐ What is the probability that it will take at least 2 senior students to find one with a driving license? Be sure to show your work.

    A   21%

    B   30%

    C   50%

    D   70%

Common Core Standard 7.SP.C.8.C – Statistics & Probability

☐ What is the probability that it will take at least 3 senior students to find one with a driving license? Be sure to show your work.

    A   6.3%

    B   7.3%

    C   9.29%

    D   10.29%

Common Core Standard 7.SP.C.8.C – Statistics & Probability

☐ What is the probability that it will take at least 4 senior students to find one without a driving license? Be sure to show your work.

    A   6.3%

    B   7.3%

    C   9.29%

    D   10.29%

©Teachers' Treasures Publishing

Name_____

ASSESSMENT

Common Core Standard 7.SP.C.8.C – Statistics & Probability

"10% of women prefer comedies"

☐ What is the probability that it will take at least 2 women to find one who prefers comedies? Be sure to show your work.

    A   7.29%

    B   8.1%

    C   9%

    D   50%

Common Core Standard 7.SP.C.8.C – Statistics & Probability

☐ What is the probability that it will take at least 3 women to find one who prefers comedies? Be sure to show your work.

    A   7.29%

    B   8.1%

    C   9%

    D   10%

Common Core Standard 7.SP.C.8.C – Statistics & Probability

☐ What is the probability that it will take at least 4 women to find one who prefers comedies? Be sure to show your work.

    A   7.29%

    B   8.1%

    C   9%

    D   10%

Name_____

ASSESSMENT

Common Core Standard 7.SP.C.8.C – Statistics & Probability

"95% of Italians have dark hair"

☐ What is the probability that it will take at least 2 Italians to find one with light hair? Be sure to show your work.

    A   0.24%

    B   4.51%

    C   4.75%

    D   5%

Common Core Standard 7.SP.C.8.C – Statistics & Probability

☐ What is the probability that it will take at least 3 Italians to find one with light hair? Be sure to show your work.

    A   0.24%

    B   4.51%

    C   4.75%

    D   5%

Common Core Standard 7.SP.C.8.C – Statistics & Probability

☐ What is the probability that it will take at least 3 Italians to find one with light hair? Be sure to show your work.

    A   0.24%

    B   4.51%

    C   4.75%

    D   5%

©Teachers' Treasures Publishing

ANSWER KEY

7.RP.A.1

Page 1 .... B, A, B
Page 2 .... C, C, B
Page 3 .... A, B, D
Page 4 .... A, B, A
Page 5 .... B, A, A
Page 6 .... C, A, B
Page 7 .... D, A, C
Page 8 .... D, D, D

7.RP.A.2.A

Page 9 .... B, A, B
Page 10 .... B, C, A
Page 11 .... C, A, B
Page 12 .... B, C, D
Page 13 .... D, C, B
Page 14 .... A, C, D
Page 15 .... C, B, A
Page 16 .... A, B, D

7.RP.A.2.B

Page 17 .... C, A, D
Page 18 .... D, A, C
Page 19 .... C, B, A
Page 20 .... B, C, A
Page 21 .... D, C, C
Page 22 .... C, B, D
Page 23 .... A, B, A
Page 24 .... C, C, C

7.RP.A.2.C

Page 25 .... C, B, A
Page 26 .... D, C, A
Page 27 .... A, C, D
Page 28 .... A, D, B
Page 29 .... C, C, C
Page 30 .... D, B, C
Page 31 .... A, C, B
Page 32 .... D, C, C

7.RP.A.2.D

Page 33 .... B, A, C
Page 34 .... B, D, A
Page 35 .... A, B, D
Page 36 .... C, C, D
Page 37 .... A, B, C
Page 38 .... B, A, D
Page 39 .... A, C, D
Page 40 .... C, C, C

7.RP.A.3

Page 41 .... B, A, C
Page 42 .... D, B, D
Page 43 .... C, B, C
Page 44 .... C, A, D
Page 45 .... C, C, B
Page 46 .... A, C, D
Page 47 .... B, C, B
Page 48 .... B, D, D

© Teachers' Treasures Publishing

ANSWER KEY

7.NS.A.1.A

Page 49 .... C, B, D
Page 50 .... C, A, A
Page 51 .... C, B, A
Page 52 .... C, A, D
Page 53 .... A, A, C
Page 54 .... B, C, B
Page 55 .... B, D, D
Page 56 .... A, D, B

7.NS.A.1.B

Page 57 .... C, D, C
Page 58 .... D, A, B
Page 59 .... D, C, A
Page 60 .... B, C, B
Page 61 .... C, D, D
Page 62 .... D, C, B
Page 63 .... C, D, C
Page 64 .... A, B, B

7.NS.A.1.C

Page 65 .... C, B, B
Page 66 .... B, D, D
Page 67 .... C, D, A
Page 68 .... A, C, D
Page 69 .... B, A, D
Page 70 .... A, C, C
Page 71 .... B, B, A
Page 72 .... A, D, C

7.NS.A.1.D

Page 73 .... D, C, A
Page 74 .... B, D, A
Page 75 .... B, C, A
Page 76 .... A, D, A
Page 77 .... C, B, A
Page 78 .... D, A, B
Page 79 .... A, C, B
Page 80 .... C, B, C

7.NS.A.2.A

Page 81 .... D, A, C
Page 82 .... D, D, A
Page 83 .... A, D, B
Page 84 .... C, B, C
Page 85 .... B, A, D
Page 86 .... B, D, C
Page 87 .... A, C, D
Page 88 .... A, B, C

7.NS.A.2.B

Page 89 .... D, B, A
Page 90 .... B, A, D
Page 91 .... B, C, B
Page 92 .... D, D, C
Page 93 .... B, C, B
Page 94 .... A, D, A
Page 95 .... B, A, D
Page 96 .... B, B, A

© Teachers' Treasures Publishing

ANSWER KEY

7.NS.A.2.C

Page 97 .... B, B, C
Page 98 .... B, D, A
Page 99 .... A, A, B
Page 100 .... C, A, D
Page 101 .... D, C, B
Page 102 .... A, C, C
Page 103 .... D, B, D
Page 104 .... B, B, A

7.NS.A.2.D

Page 105 .... C, A, D
Page 106 .... B, B, D
Page 107 .... D, D, A
Page 108 .... D, C, A
Page 109 .... D, B, C
Page 110 .... D, B, D
Page 111 .... D, C, A
Page 112 .... D, A, C

7.NS.A.3

Page 113 .... B, B, D
Page 114 .... A, C, C
Page 115 .... D, D, B
Page 116 .... B, B, D
Page 117 .... D, D, B
Page 118 .... D, C, D
Page 119 .... A, A, A
Page 120 .... C, A, A

7.EE.A.1

Page 121 .... C, A, B
Page 122 .... B, B, C
Page 123 .... C, B, C
Page 124 .... A, D, D
Page 125 .... D, C, D
Page 126 .... A, C, A
Page 127 .... C, B, B
Page 128 .... A, D, A

7.EE.A.2

Page 129 .... B, D, A
Page 130 .... C, A, D
Page 131 .... B, B, D
Page 132 .... B, A, A
Page 133 .... D, A, D
Page 134 .... B, B, A
Page 135 .... C, D, C
Page 136 .... A, B, C

7.EE.B.3

Page 137 .... A, C, C
Page 138 .... B, C, D
Page 139 .... A, D, C
Page 140 .... C, C, A
Page 141 .... A, B, B
Page 142 .... B, B, C
Page 143 .... B, A, B
Page 144 .... C, B, D

ANSWER KEY

7.EE.B.4.A

Page 145 .... D, D, C
Page 146 .... C, B, A
Page 147 .... A, B, A
Page 148 .... C, D, B
Page 149 .... B, D, B
Page 150 .... B, D, A
Page 151 .... D, D, C
Page 152 .... B, A, A

7.EE.B.4.B

Page 153 .... C, C, B
Page 154 .... A, B, B
Page 155 .... A, A, C
Page 156 .... D, D, C
Page 157 .... C, B, D
Page 158 .... A, D, B
Page 159 .... A, B, C
Page 160 .... B, A, C

7.G.A.1

Page 161 .... D, B, A
Page 162 .... B, C, D
Page 163 .... B, D, D
Page 164 .... D, C, B
Page 165 .... C, B, B
Page 166 .... B, B, C
Page 167 .... D, C, B
Page 168 .... C, A, D

7.G.A.2

Page 169 .... B, A, D
Page 170 .... B, B, A
Page 171 .... B, B, A
Page 172 .... B, A, B
Page 173 .... B, A, D
Page 174 .... A, A, A
Page 175 .... A, A, B
Page 176 .... B, D, A

7.G.A.3

Page 177 .... B, D, C
Page 178 .... A, D, B
Page 179 .... A, C, D
Page 180 .... A, B, A
Page 181 .... A, D, A
Page 182 .... B, C, A
Page 183 .... A, A, C
Page 184 .... D, B, A

7.G.B.4

Page 185 .... A, C, D
Page 186 .... D, B, A
Page 187 .... B, A, A
Page 188 .... C, B, C
Page 189 .... A, A, B
Page 190 .... C, B, B
Page 191 .... A, B, B
Page 192 .... C, A, C

© Teachers' Treasures Publishing

ANSWER KEY

7.G.B.5

Page 193	A, B, C
Page 194	B, A, A
Page 195	C, A, C
Page 196	B, B, D
Page 197	A, C, C
Page 198	B, B, C
Page 199	D, D, B
Page 200	C, C, B

7.G.B.6

Page 201	D, D, C
Page 202	B, C, A
Page 203	A, A, B
Page 204	B, D, C
Page 205	C, C, C
Page 206	B, D, D
Page 207	B, D, C
Page 208	C, A, C

7.SP.A.1

Page 209	A, A, B
Page 210	C, C, B
Page 211	B, C, A
Page 212	B, A, A
Page 213	A, C, A
Page 214	C, A, A
Page 215	C, C, A
Page 216	B, B, A

7.SP.A.2

Page 217	C, B, D
Page 218	A, B, A
Page 219	C, C, A
Page 220	B, C, B
Page 221	B, C, A
Page 222	C, D, D
Page 223	B, A, D
Page 224	A, C, D

7.SP.B.3

Page 225	A, B, D
Page 226	D, B, A
Page 227	D, C, C
Page 228	B, C, C
Page 229	C, D, C
Page 230	C, D, C
Page 231	B, B, C
Page 232	D, C, C

7.SP.B.4

Page 233	D, C, A
Page 234	C, D, A
Page 235	C, D, B
Page 236	C, D, A
Page 237	A, B, D
Page 238	C, D, A
Page 239	A, B, A
Page 240	B, A, D

© Teachers' Treasures Publishing

ANSWER KEY

7.SP.C.5

Page 241 .... C, B, A
Page 242 .... B, C, C
Page 243 .... B, B, C
Page 244 .... C, C, A
Page 245 .... C, A, B
Page 246 .... A, C, C
Page 247 .... A, A, C
Page 248 .... C, C, B

7.SP.C.6

Page 249 .... A, A, B
Page 250 .... B, B, A
Page 251 .... C, D, B
Page 252 .... B, C, B
Page 253 .... A, C, C
Page 254 .... D, D, A
Page 255 .... C, C, B
Page 256 .... D, C, C

7.SP.C.7.A

Page 257 .... D, A, A
Page 258 .... D, B, C
Page 259 .... A, B, D
Page 260 .... B, D, B
Page 261 .... B, D, B
Page 262 .... B, D, C
Page 263 .... D, C, D
Page 264 .... B, D, A

7.SP.C.7.B

Page 265 .... D, A, B
Page 266 .... C, A, B
Page 267 .... B, A, D
Page 268 .... A, B, D
Page 269 .... B, A, D
Page 270 .... A, D, B
Page 271 .... B, A, C
Page 272 .... C, A, D

7.SP.C.8.A

Page 273 .... C, D, B
Page 274 .... A, C, B
Page 275 .... A, B, D
Page 276 .... C, B, D
Page 277 .... D, B, A
Page 278 .... D, B, A
Page 279 .... D, C, B
Page 280 .... B, D, A

7.SP.C.8.B

Page 281 .... D, B, D
Page 282 .... C, D, B
Page 283 .... B, D, A
Page 284 .... B, D, A
Page 285 .... D, D, B
Page 286 .... D, D, D
Page 287 .... D, D, B
Page 288 .... C, B, D

ANSWER KEY

7.SP.C.8.C

Page 289 .... C, A, A
Page 290 .... B, B, C
Page 291 .... C, B, A
Page 292 .... C, A, B
Page 293 .... C, A, B
Page 294 .... A, A, D
Page 295 .... C, B, A
Page 296 .... C, B, A